Y0-BUP-111

A15046 667108

RAND

A\System Description of the Heroin Trade /

Michael Childress

Prepared for the
United States Army
RAND's Drug Policy Research Center

HV
5822
.H4
C48
1994
West

Arroyo Center
Drug Policy Research Center

Arizona State Univ. West Library

Approved for public release; distribution unlimited

Arizona State Univ. West Library

Preface

This report describes and discusses applications for a computer spreadsheet–based, comprehensive "system description" of the quantity and flow of heroin from initial cultivation and processing, through international transportation, to domestic distribution and consumption. RAND has developed and documented similar system descriptions for cocaine and marijuana. This effort is being jointly sponsored by RAND's Arroyo Center and Drug Policy Research Center. The study should be of interest to policymakers and analysts supporting the National Drug Control Program at the national level and others involved in resource allocation for, or analysis of, the drug problem.

The Arroyo Center

The Arroyo Center is the U.S. Army's federally funded research and development center (FFRDC) for studies and analysis operated by RAND. The Arroyo Center provides the Army with objective, independent analytic research on major policy and organizational concerns, emphasizing mid- and long-term problems. Its research is carried out in four programs: Strategy and Doctrine; Force Development and Technology; Military Logistics; and Manpower and Training.

Army Regulation 5-21 contains basic policy for the conduct of the Arroyo Center. The Army provides continuing guidance and oversight through the Arroyo Center Policy Committee (ACPC), which is co-chaired by the Vice Chief of Staff and by the Assistant Secretary for Research, Development, and Acquisition. Arroyo Center work is performed under contract MDA903-91-C-0006.

The Arroyo Center is housed in RAND's Army Research Division. RAND is a private, nonprofit institution that conducts analytic research on a wide range of public policy matters affecting the nation's security and welfare.

James T. Quinlivan is Vice President for the Army Research Division and Director of the Arroyo Center. Those interested in further information about the Arroyo Center should contact his office directly:

James T. Quinlivan
RAND
1700 Main Street
P.O. Box 2138
Santa Monica CA 90407-2138

The Drug Policy Research Center

The Drug Policy Research Center (DPRC) is supported by the Ford and Weingart Foundations. This work is part of the Center's extensive and ongoing assessment of drug problems at local and national levels. Audrey Burnam and Jonathan Caulkins are the Co-Directors of the DPRC. Those interested in further information about the DPRC should contact their offices directly. Audrey Burnam may be contacted at the above address; Jonathan Caulkins may be contacted at the following address:

RAND
2100 M Street, NW
Washington, D.C. 20037-1270

Contents

Figures

viii

Tables

Summary

The United States has devoted substantial resources toward stemming the flow of illegal drugs. Yet it is difficult to accurately characterize the drug system, given that the production and trafficking of drugs are illegal enterprises cloaked in secrecy. While it is generally not possible to validate the basic parameters of the drug trade, a better understanding may help policymakers, law enforcement agencies, and analysts to evaluate and execute effective responses to the drug problem.

Purpose

A comprehensive accounting framework for estimating the quantities and flows of drugs would go a long way toward such an understanding. To this end, RAND has developed—and this report documents—a computer spreadsheet–based "system description" for the heroin trade. This system description serves as a database and an analytical tool. It consists of four interrelated spreadsheets—a database and three others that mirror the general pattern of the heroin trade: production, transportation, and U.S. distribution. The database provides primarily production-related data from 1985 through 1991. This report also provides detailed information on how to use the model. The spreadsheets are available for either IBM (DOS) or Apple-based machines upon request to RAND.

Approach and Application

Using information available in the open literature, we constructed an end-to-end description of the heroin trade with an emphasis on quantities entering the United States. Despite the fact that data are limited, we were able to tell a reasonably comprehensive story. The system framework has allowed us (and any other user) to pool information from various sources while imposing consistency on these disparate data.

To examine the potential utility of this tool, this report details three distinct but related applications: improving the estimation processes, conducting sensitivity analyses, and guiding planning and assessment. In improving the estimation process, an analyst can use the comprehensive framework to evaluate assumptions or data in terms of their downstream effects on other indicators. For example, it is possible to determine the likely downstream effects of an increase in opium crop yields on the estimated amount of heroin shipped to the United States. Sensitivity analysis can be used to understand the import of certain parameters versus others (this may be helpful in allocating intelligence resources, for example) and to evaluate first-order effects of change in the system, such as an eradication program.

Acknowledgments

The author is grateful to RAND colleagues Bonnie Dombey-Moore, Susan Resetar, and Peter Reuter who, through their research on the cocaine system, paved the way and made this author's work much easier. Karyn Model provided a thoughtful and comprehensive review and Deborah Elms assisted in document preparation.

1. Introduction

Background

The priority afforded to reducing illegal drug use in the United States increased considerably during the 1980s. This emphasis is evidenced by federal spending on antidrug efforts, which increased from $1.5 billion in 1981 to a projected $12.7 billion in 1993, an increase of nearly 750 percent.[1] However, even this increase in federal expenditures may present only a partial picture, because some previously purchased resources have also shifted to the drug war. The U.S. military's increasing role in antidrug efforts is a prime example.

The foundation for the U.S. military's involvement in the drug war was laid in 1981 when Congress amended the *Posse Comitatus* Act of 1878, paving the way for the military to assist civilian law enforcement agencies in the drug war.[2] By the late 1980s, illegal drug trafficking was declared a threat to U.S. national security,[3] and Congress had expanded the military's role in the drug war by mandating that the Department of Defense (DoD) play a leading role in at least four broad areas: (1) equipment loans, (2) training of law enforcement agency officials, (3) radar coverage of major drug trafficking routes, and (4) intelligence gathering and dissemination.[4]

Despite all the resources dedicated to stemming the illegal flow of drugs, the basic data and analytical tools available to decisionmakers have important gaps and limitations. For example, the government neither systematically estimates basic quantities of cocaine and heroin consumed nor assesses the impacts of different drug control programs.

---

[1]Office of National Drug Control Policy (ONDCP), June 1992, p. 8. There was nearly a 400 percent increase from 1981 to 1989. See Carpenter and Rouse (1990), p. 2.

[2]The *Posse Comitatus* Act of 1878 prohibited the use of the military for civilian law enforcement. See U.S. Congress, House Committee on the Judiciary (1981).

[3]President Reagan signed a National Security Decision Directive (NSDD) in April of 1986 stating that the drug trade is a threat to the national security of the United States. See Richburg (1986).

[4]United States General Accounting Office (1987), p. 2.

Limitations of Current Information About the Drug Trade

The inadequacies of current data on the production, transportation, and consumption of illegal drugs frustrate analysts and policymakers alike in their attempts to understand the rudiments of illegal drug activities. It will always be difficult to obtain good data on an inherently clandestine activity. Complicating matters further, opium cultivation and heroin production occur in many areas of the world that are remote, inhospitable, and perhaps inaccessible for political reasons.[5] Basic information, such as the number of hectares under cultivation, the level of indigenous opium consumption, or the amount converted to heroin for export, is difficult, if not impossible, to obtain. These data problems exacerbate the difficulty of making reasonable choices on how to allocate scarce resources directed at reducing the problem, not to mention the task of measuring the effectiveness of chosen policies.

The two major sources of unclassified production data are the *International Narcotics Control Strategy Report* (INCSR), produced by the U.S. State Department's Bureau of International Narcotics Matters (INM), and *The NNICC Report* (formerly published as *The Narcotics Intelligence Estimate* or *NIE*), generated by an interagency group headed by the Drug Enforcement Agency (DEA).

Basic production estimates from these documents, such as opium production data, have shown persistent differences.[6] Figure 1.1 shows the high and low estimates from the INCSR and NNICC from 1983 to 1989.[7] For opium production, the NNICC estimates have been consistently higher than the INCSR estimates.[8] The differences between their midpoints have been as low as 0.5 percent in 1985 and as high as 11.2 percent in 1987. Also, while the INCSR has typically offered a point estimate, the range between the high and low NNICC estimates has been generally increasing since 1985.

---

[5]For example, Iran, Burma, Afghanistan, and Lebanon are major producers of illicit opium, and these countries have recently experienced internal turmoil or have governments unfriendly to the United States. The other principal producers are Thailand, Laos, Pakistan, Mexico, and Guatemala (with a potentially burgeoning production in Colombia).

[6]In 1990 the NNICC began publishing the INCSR numbers as the formal government estimate. However, there are still fundamental disagreements within and between these two groups (interview with a Defense Intelligence Agency analyst, May 1992).

[7]These estimates are for the six major producers of opium: Afghanistan, Iran, Pakistan, Burma, Laos, Thailand, and Mexico.

[8]The same is true for cocaine; see Dombey-Moore, Resetar, and Childress (forthcoming), p. 2.

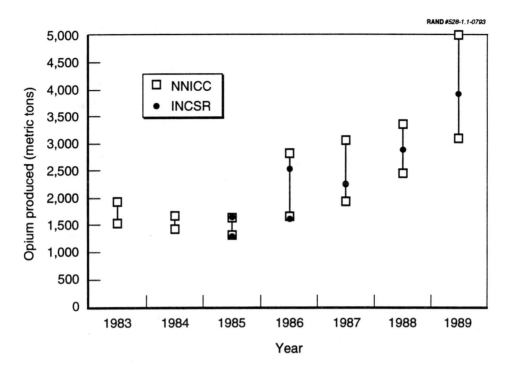

**Figure 1.1—Worldwide Opium Production: NNICC and INCSR Estimates
from 1983 to 1989**

Other discrepancies occur as well. There are occasional revisions in the
published data from year to year—some with explanation,[9] and some without
explanation.[10] There are also disagreements among the NNICC's participating
agencies.[11] And the discrepancies are even greater for other drugs.[12] All of the
above indicate the general uncertainty surrounding some fundamental estimates
of drug production.

---

[9]For example, opium yield estimates for Burma and Thailand were recently decreased by 28
percent after a study indicated that lower estimates were warranted. See INCSR, 1992, p. 29.

[10]Peter Reuter and David Ronfeldt (1992, p. 54) point out that "in 1980, the NNICC estimated
Mexican opium production at barely 10 metric tons; one year later, the 1980 estimate was revised
upward by between 50 and 60 percent, with little or no explanation." These problems of estimation
occur with Mexico, a country that is contiguous to the United States, has good relations across the
border, and is not experiencing war or any other type of internal turmoil. By contrast, deriving
estimates for Southeast or Southwest Asian production is much more difficult.

[11]The 1989 *NNICC Report* estimates that Afghanistan's opium production was from 460 to 710
metric tons. However, the DEA believes that a better estimate is 700 to 800 metric tons. See the 1989
NNICC Report, p. 49.

[12]See Dombey-Moore, Resetar, and Childress (forthcoming) and Reuter and Ronfeldt (1992) for
a discussion of marijuana production estimates for Mexico.

The uncertainties about heroin production estimates compound the difficulty of determining heroin consumption in the United States. For example, worldwide heroin production has been steadily increasing since 1985, as illustrated in Figure 1.2.[13] This rise in worldwide heroin production, coupled with U.S. domestic indicators on heroin availability, such as the increasing availability of heroin in America's high schools,[14] additional heroin seizures,[15] rising purity levels,[16] and decreasing price,[17] seems to indicate that heroin availability (and maybe consumption) is rising.[18]

At the same time, however, heroin consumption indicators do not reflect a strong surge in usage.[19] As Figure 1.3 shows, the percentage of the population from 18

---

[13]The estimated worldwide heroin production is generated by the spreadsheet model described in this report. The model takes into account opium production by the world's major producers: Afghanistan, Iran, Pakistan, Burma, Laos, Thailand, Mexico, Guatemala, and Lebanon. The model generates an estimate of gross heroin production before losses, seizures, and consumption within the producing country. We did not depict yearly estimates of metric tons of heroin produced, because such estimates are likely to be too high; greater amounts of opium are consumed than are accounted for in the model. A lot of opium is not converted to heroin but is consumed as opium. We have relied upon the INCSR and NNICC reports for estimates of producing-country opium consumption, although they appear to be exceedingly low. Indeed, in some cases there is no reported opium consumption in countries that are widely believed to be net importers of opium to satiate domestic demand. As a result, we have emphasized through Figure 1.2 the annual trend, or annual percentage change since 1985, rather than the estimated *absolute* amount of heroin produced.

[14]For example, the 1990 annual High School Survey of the nation's high school seniors revealed that cocaine and marijuana were becoming less available (7 percent decrease) between 1988 and 1990, while heroin was becoming more available (7 percent increase). The 1991 data indicate that heroin was becoming less available (2 percent decrease since 1988), but was practically stable compared to the reductions in cocaine (17 percent decrease) and marijuana (12 percent decrease) availability since 1988. See *National Drug Control Strategy*, The White House, January 1992, pp. 24–25.

[15]According to the DEA, heroin seizures in the United States have increased by over 200 percent between 1981 and 1988; from 1987 to 1988, seizures doubled from 382.4 kilograms (kg) to 793.9 kg. The Federal-Wide Drug Seizure System (FDSS) indicates that 1,095.2 kgs were seized in 1989; 813.9 in 1990; and 1,376.4 in 1991. These are seizures made within the jurisdiction of the United States by the Drug Enforcement Administration, Federal Bureau of Investigation, U.S. Customs Service, and U.S. Coast Guard.

[16]The average purity level on the street for the user has gone from an average of 3 to 5 percent in the early 1980s to as high as 50 percent in some cities by the end of the 1980s. The average purity level across the country is currently about 30 percent. See U.S. Congress, House of Representatives (1990), p. 38. Also, refer to U.S. Department of Justice, Drug Enforcement Administration, Office of Intelligence, "From the Source to the Street: Mid-1990 Prices for Cannabis, Cocaine, and Heroin," *Intelligence Trends*, various issues; and U.S. Department of Justice, Drug Enforcement Administration, Office of Intelligence, "An Annual Report of the Source Areas, Cost, and Purity of Retail-Level Heroin," *Domestic Monitor Program*, various issues.

[17]The price of heroin decreased by more than half during the 1980s. See U.S. Congress, House of Representatives (1990), p. 38.

[18]A complete discussion of the various trends is provided in BOTEC Analysis Corporation (1992).

[19]Obtaining accurate data on heroin use is problematic for a variety of reasons. For example, the major instrument for collecting data on the drug-using population is the National Household Survey, and many drug users do not reside in households. Some heroin users, however, are functional members of society. According to Dr. Robert B. Millman, director of drug and alcohol abuse programs at New York Hospital–Payne Whitney Psychiatric Clinic, "there are enormous numbers of people in all walks of life who have integrated heroin use with their lives." See Treaster (July 22, 1992), p. 1.

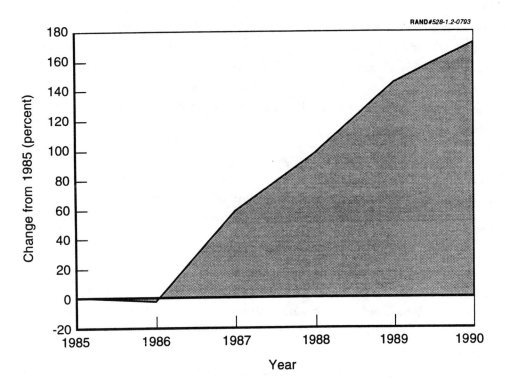

Figure 1.2—Estimated Worldwide Heroin Production

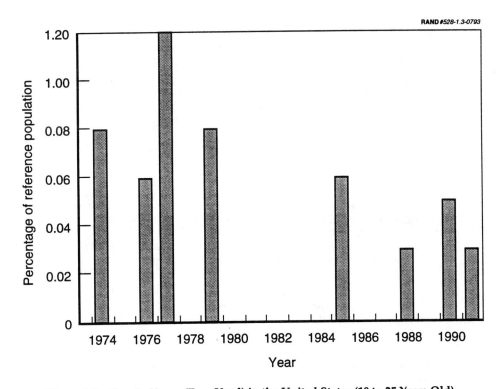

Figure 1.3—Heroin Usage (Ever Used) in the United States (18 to 25 Years Old)

6

to 25 years old that reports taking heroin is not increasing dramatically.[20] Also, heroin-related emergency room visits, as captured by the Drug Abuse Warning Network (DAWN), decreased from 1988 to 1990.[21] Moreover, because of a societal intolerance of drug use in general, heroin use in particular, and a lack of new initiates, some believe that the United States is *not* on the cusp of a new heroin epidemic.[22]

Given the uncertainty that surrounds the basic data on the outlines of the heroin trade, it is not surprising that there are occasionally very different estimates for the same factor or estimates for two different factors that appear to be incompatible with each other. The model described in this report can be used as a tool to help manage these problems.

Since the drug trade is a "system," it is impossible to end up with more heroin than the sum of the raw materials with which it was produced.[23] By economic reasoning, there should also be some relationship between prevalence or amount of drug consumed and the amount of drug produced or imported. The "system description" imposes a framework that either forces consistency in assumptions or data or highlights sources of inconsistency. Essentially then, it is an elaborate accounting scheme for reconciling estimates of the quantities and flows of heroin.

Purpose

This study describes a tool to assist decisionmakers and analysts in estimating quantities and charting the flow of heroin. The tool is a computer spreadsheet–based model which provides a system description of the heroin trade. Along with a database, the model contains other spreadsheets that mirror the general pattern of the heroin trade: production, international transportation, and U.S.

---

[20]These data are from National Institute on Drug Abuse (NIDA), National Household Survey on Drug Abuse, and represent the percentage of 18 to 25 year old adults who have "ever used" heroin. Similar data on usage in the last 30 days is unavailable for heroin. This figure shows the data for the 18 to 25 year old group because the data for the other age groups are unavailable.

[21]The average number of DAWN-related incidents per quarter was 3,813 in 1988; 3,756 in 1989; and 2,984 in the first two quarters of 1990. See *National Drug Control Strategy*, The White House, February 1991, p. 85. Annual figures on the national level show a less dramatic downturn. For example, 38,063 incidents were reported in 1988; 41,656 in 1989; 33,576 in 1990; and 36,576 in 1991. Refer to U.S. Department of Health and Human Services (1992), p. 10. However, this is a recent downturn because the number of heroin-related DAWN incidents increased at a steady rate from 1980 to 1988, with 12,522 in 1985 and 15,733 in 1988.

[22]See ONDCP (1992).

[23]This is meant as a general statement. During a particular time period, some final product could come from storage and not from the raw materials of that period.

distribution. The model is designed to allow users to substitute their own data or assumptions about parameters.[24]

Outline

Section 2 provides a narrative account of opium cultivation and heroin production. The section provides some information about the underlying process modeled in the spreadsheets. Section 3 gives a general systems overview of the model; Section 4 discusses some possible applications the model could support; and Section 5 is the conclusion. Appendix A lists the regional organization of the United States used in the spreadsheets; Appendices B and C provide more detailed information about the structure and operation of the spreadsheet model; Appendix D presents a short primer on the INCSR's data collection methodology; and Appendix E displays the output from a simulation to test for the effect of propagating errors in the model.

_____

[24]Similar system descriptions have been developed at RAND for cocaine and marijuana.

2. The Heroin Production Process

This section provides a brief overview of the heroin production and transportation processes that underlie the spreadsheet model. It describes the steps in the process, the conversion factors as processing moves from stage to stage, and some of the uncertainties surrounding these factors. It also summarizes the roles of various countries in the production and transportation of heroin.

The first subsection provides a generic description of how heroin is produced, describing the stages, ingredients, equipment, and time required for the various stages. But the description is notional in the sense that it does not take into account any production differences that may occur in any of the heroin-producing countries. It also treats the process as though it took place in a single location with no interruptions, even though this is rarely the case. The second subsection describes the uncertainty over some basic estimates of heroin production.

Producing Heroin

How It Is Made

Manufacturing heroin (diacetylmorphine) from the opium poppy plant (*Papaver somniferum L.*) is a surprisingly uncomplicated three-step process. The primary raw material is opium, which is harvested from the poppy plant, and the two intermediate products are morphine base and heroin base.[1] It requires about 10 kg of opium to produce about 1 kg of morphine base, which in turn yields about the same amount of heroin base and heroin. However, the yields at each stage can vary widely depending upon the availability and quality of equipment and chemicals, as well as the skill and sophistication of the "chemist."

The opium poppy plant is an extremely adaptable and hardy plant, but does best in tropical and semitropical temperate zones. If growing conditions are ideal, two opium harvests per year can be obtained from the plant. The unripe seed capsules are incised, releasing a milky juice which is gathered and dried to form

---

[1]Morphine base is also known as No. 1 heroin, and heroin base is sometimes referred to as No. 2 heroin.

brown raw opium. This raw opium can be consumed as such and indeed is consumed in great quantities in many producing countries.

The processing of heroin requires opium, water, lime, a pH modifier, and an acetylating agent. Except for the acetylating agent, all of these materials are widely available where opium is grown. There are numerous processing methods, each somewhat different.[2] Nevertheless, each method entails soaking, heating, and filtering the opium until a brown powder is achieved. This power is compressed into bricks, and is known as morphine base.

There is little variation in the procedures used to convert morphine base into heroin. The dried morphine base is mixed with acetic anhydride or some other acetylating agent, heated to a boil, cooled, and mixed with water. After the resulting solution is filtered, a second solution of water and sodium carbonate is added to the heroin acetate, and the combination is filtered and then dried. This process results in the powdery gray No. 2 heroin or heroin base. However, this is an intermediate step. Heroin base is insoluble in water and therefore unsuitable for injection.

Further refinement of the heroin base results in the two marketable products, No. 3 heroin, sometimes called smoking heroin, a soluble salt-like substance that is usually gray or brown, and No. 4 heroin, the purest form of heroin, usually a fluffy white powder. Since the mid-1980s, Mexican black tar heroin has become increasingly available in the United States.[3] Mexican heroin is produced as a brown powder or a black tar, mostly the latter.[4] The production process used to produce black tar heroin is a cruder, shortcut version of the method used to produce the traditional Mexican brown powder.[5] Typically, Mexican black tar heroin is a hydrochloride salt and is injected.[6]

---

[2]For a technical description of the conversion process refer to Cooper (1989). For a discussion oriented toward the average layperson, see Krivanek (1988), pp. 105–106.

[3]U.S. Department of Justice, (1986).

[4]U.S. Department of Justice, (1991), p. 1.

[5]Many contaminants, like plant by-products, are not removed, indicating inadequate filtering methods and laboratory conditions. U.S. Department of Justice (1986), p. 5.

[6]*Domestic Monitor Program*, U.S. Department of Justice, DEA, Office of Intelligence, July 1992, p. 85. Black tar heroin is typically high in purity, brown to black in color, and sticky like roofing tar or hard like coal. See *Domestic Monitor Program*, U.S. Department of Justice, DEA, Office of Intelligence, October 1992, p. 39. At the street level, a gram of tar heroin with an average purity of 40 percent sold for $150 to $400 a few years ago. By contrast, a gram of Mexican brown or Southeast Asian heroin with an average purity of 17 percent went for $80 to $450, and a gram of Southwest Asian heroin with an average purity of 10 percent sold for $80 to $450. See U.S. Department of Justice (1991), pp. 21–25.

10

Who Does What?

There are three major illicit opium production regions: the Golden Triangle countries of Southeast Asia (Burma, Thailand, and Laos), the Golden Crescent countries of Southwest Asia (Pakistan, Afghanistan, and Iran), and Mexico. As Figure 2.1 illustrates, the countries of Southeast Asia (SEA) are the major producers of opium, especially since the mid-1980s, having supplanted the Southwest Asian (SWA) producers.[7]

The percentage distribution for the largest producing countries in 1991 is presented in Fig. 2.2. The 1991 opium production estimates (in metric tons) for Burma, Afghanistan, Iran, and Laos accounted for just over 90 percent of the

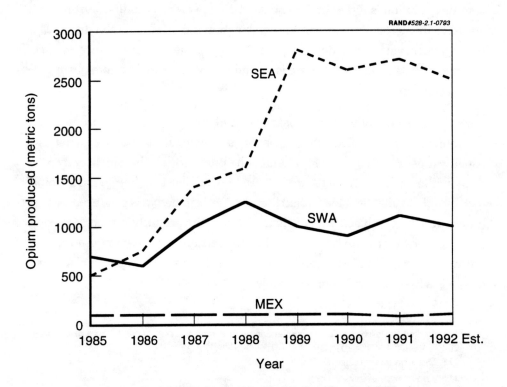

RAND#528-2.1-0793

Figure 2.1—The World's Three Principal Opium Producing Regions

---

[7]These data are from various editions of the *International Narcotics Control Strategy Report (INCSR)*. There is considerable uncertainty regarding these production estimates. According to the 1991 *INCSR*, the most reliable data are for the number of hectares under cultivation, because these data can be collected through satellite reconnaissance. Unfortunately, crop yields and conversion factors in the production process are subject to many variables for which there is little or no information. Consequently, these factors are difficult to estimate with precision. For a discussion of the methodology, see Appendix D or the *INCSR*, March 1991, pp. 7–8.

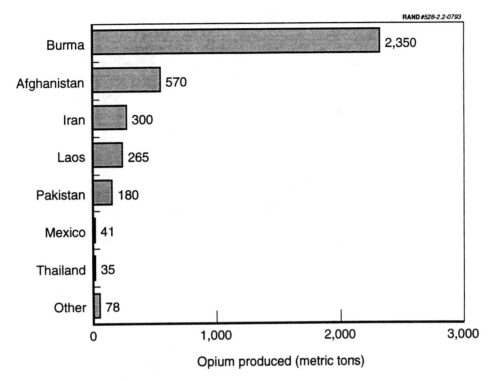

RAND #528-2.2-0793

Figure 2.2—Opium Production by the Major Producing Countries in 1991

world's illicit opium.[8] In addition to the countries already mentioned, other producing countries include Lebanon, Guatemala, and Colombia.[9]

Heroin production does not necessarily occur solely in the country that cultivates the opium. For example, while Burma produces most of the world's opium, much is sent to Malaysia and Thailand for further refinement. Moreover, a lot of heroin production has been moved from other Asian countries to Laos, where the authorities are less vigorous in their attempts to eliminate heroin refinement. Other significant producers of illicit heroin reside in India and Turkey, countries that have substantial licit opium cultivation and the technical sophistication for converting it to morphine or heroin. Several countries serve as important transshipment points as the heroin moves from Asia to the world's markets; these countries include Hong Kong, Malaysia, Nepal, Nigeria, Philippines, Singapore, and Turkey. Table 2.1 lists the countries involved in the heroin trade and briefly summarizes their major roles.

---

[8]*INCSR*, March 1992, p. 28. India is the world's major producer of *licit* opium for pharmaceutical purposes.

[9]The opium poppy plant is not native to Colombia, but in early 1991, Colombian government officials discovered several hectares of poppy under cultivation. In May 1991, the first Colombia-grown heroin was seized in the United States at New York's Kennedy International Airport by Customs officials. See Treaster (January 14, 1992), p. A10.

Table 2.1

Illicit Heroin Trade Countries at a Glance

Country	Primary Roles	Cultivation	Eradication	Opiate Use
Afghanistan	Cultivation, processing[a]	Illegal	None	Unknown
Burma	Cultivation, processing	Illegal[b]	No aerial spraying	50,000 to 150,000[c]
Colombia	Cultivation, processing	Illegal	Yes	Low
Guatemala	Cultivation	Illegal	Yes	Low[d]
Hong Kong	Transit[e]	None	N.A.	10 meteric tons/year
India	Cultivation, processing, transit	Legal[f]	Yes	5 million users
Iran	Cultivation, processing, transit	Illegal (unknown hectares)	Unknown	2 million users
Laos	Cultivation, processing[g]	Illegal	Minimal	Widespread
Lebanon	Cultivation, transit	Illegal	Minimal	Unknown
Malaysia	Processing,[h] transit[i]	None	N.A.	Widespread
Mexico	Cultivation, processing[j]	Illegal	Yes	Low[d]
Nepal	Transit[k]	None	N.A.	25,000 users
Nigeria	Transit[l]	None	N.A.	Rising
Pakistan	Cultivation, processing,[m] transit	Illegal	Yes	High[n]
Philippines	Transit	None	N.A.	Low
Singapore	Transit[o]	None	N.A.	Unknown
Syria	Processing,[p] transit	None	N.A.	Unknown
Thailand	Cultivation, processing,[q] transit[r]	Illegal	Yes	High[n]
Turkey	Processing,[s] transit[t]	Legal	N.A.	Low

Table 2.1—continued

[a]There have been reports of a movement of heroin labs from Pakistan to Afghanistan because of the Pakistan government's efforts to find and destroy heroin labs on its territory.

[b]Opium cultivation is illegal in Burma, but it is believed that the Burmese government gives tacit approval to drug production.

[c]There are an estimated 50,000 to 150,000 drug addicts in Burma. Most of these are addicted to opiates.

[d]Mexican and Guatemalan nationals consume practically no opium, morphine, or heroin.

[e]Hong Kong is a major transit point for Southeast Asian heroin bound for the United States and Canada.

[f]There is believed to be illicit heroin production from illegal diversion of legally produced opium.

[g]Laos is a major refiner of opium into heroin. In fact, because of pressure in other countries, many refining operations have moved to Laos because the authorities do not seek and destroy laboratories with the same vigor.

[h]A lot of Burmese opiates are sent to Malaysia for conversion at heroin refineries along the Thailand-Malaysia border.

[i]Malaysia is a significant site for the importation, processing, and trafficking of Southeast Asian heroin.

[j]Most of the opium grown in Guatemala is shipped to Mexico, where it is processed into heroin.

[k]Nepal is increasingly becoming a transit point for heroin smuggling. Heroin moves overland from Burma to Nepal via India.

[l]Nigeria is assuming an increasingly important role as a transshipment point. Nigerian traffickers usually receive their heroin in Pakistan or Thailand, but some comes from India as well.

[m]The traditional outlets for drugs produced in Afghanistan are Pakistan and Iran. Usually, the raw opium is moved to Pakistan where it is processed.

[n]Thailand and Pakistan are thought to be net importers of opium/heroin to meet the needs of their opiate addicts. There are an estimated 260,000 to 1 million opium addicts in Pakistan.

[o]A considerable amount of Burmese heroin is believed to travel through Singapore.

[p]It is believed that much of the opium grown in Lebanon is shipped to Syria, where it is processed into heroin.

[q]Most of the opium grown in Burma is moved to Thailand for refinement. Also, some morphine base is moved from Burma to Thailand to be processed into heroin.

[r]Thailand is the major route for the Golden Triangle countries to move their heroin to world markets.

[s]Turkey has several refiners along its border with Iran that process Iranian opiates.

[t]Turkey is a major transshipment country for Southwest Asian heroin to Europe.

14

The DEA's Heroin Signature Program (HSP)[10] offers some insight into which countries are the major suppliers of heroin to the United States.[11] The HSP data illustrated in Figure 2.3 show the increasing share of SEA heroin in the United States. In 1991, 21 percent of the exhibits were of Mexican origin, 21 percent Southwest Asian, and 58 percent Southeast Asian.[12]

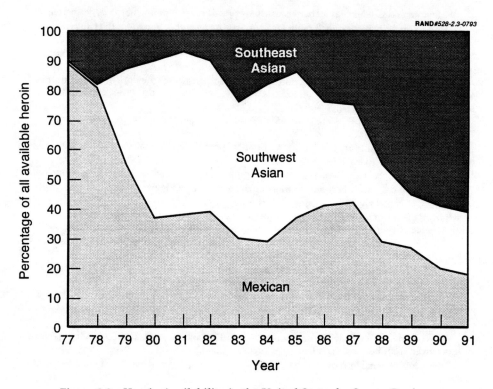

Figure 2.3—Heroin Availability in the United States by Source Region

---

[10]The DEA attempts to identify the source region of heroin in the United States with the Heroin Signature Program. A chemical analysis is performed on seized and purchased heroin to identify selected heroin characteristics and secondary constituents. Heroin exhibits are then classified according to the heroin production process, which is generally unique to the source region. Based on the exhibits analyzed, percentages of the total U.S. supply are assigned to either SEA, SWA, or MEX. There is, unfortunately, no assessment of how representative these samples are of the total amount of heroin coming into the United States. Also, one should be aware that the HSP percentages most frequently cited are based on *the number of sample exhibits*. The DEA performs a similar calculation weighted by sample size. The percentages can be strikingly different when calculated on the basis of weight. For example, the published HSP percentages based on the number of samples for 1991 are 58 percent SEA, 21 percent SWA, and 21 percent MEX. When these percentages are recalculated on the basis of the weight of the samples, the percentages change drastically to 88 percent SEA, 9 percent SWA, and 3 percent MEX. There is no a priori reason to expect that one method is a better representation of reality. In all our discussions of the HSP, we use the percentages derived from the number of samples, because these are the most commonly cited percentages.

[11]It has been estimated that roughly 6 percent of the world's illicit opiate consumption occurs in the United States. See ONDCP (1992). The estimated breakdown, which is open to debate, has Asia and the Pacific consuming 72 percent, Europe 18 percent, United States 6 percent, and 4 percent to other regions or countries.

[12]See BOTEC Analysis Corporation (1992), Appendix A, Table 22. The 1991 data were obtained from DEA personnel in Washington, D.C.

Uncertainty on Producing Estimates

Considerable uncertainty surrounds many of the estimates on opium and heroin production. The sources of some of the data are subject to bias, and there are numerous gaps in the information. The most basic estimate, the number of hectares under cultivation, is probably the most reliable, since this estimate can be obtained through aerial and satellite surveillance. However, serious problems are associated with the estimating procedure after this point.

The United States depends heavily on the governments of the opium/heroin producing countries for eradication and seizure data, and these numbers cannot be wholly accepted. For example, the U.S. government relies on the Government of Burma (GOB) for eradication and seizure data,[13] but it also views the GOB as closely associated with drug producers and traffickers.[14] In addition to the difficulties of potentially biased data, basic data do not even exist for some countries.

For instance, there are no eradication data for Afghanistan and hardly any data on Iran. Moreover, it is generally acknowledged that opium consumption is extremely high in many of the producing countries like Laos, Pakistan, and Iran. Yet neither the INCSR or the NNICC offer estimates on how much opium or heroin is consumed in these countries. Also, no attempt is made to ascertain the value of conversion factors at the intermediate production steps, and so the estimated values for heroin (Nos. 3 and 4) subsume estimated conversion factors for morphine base (No. 1) and heroin base (No. 2). All of this highlights the difficulty of deriving solid estimates on basic factors of the heroin trade.

In the face of this uncertainty, a certain arbitrariness begins to creep into the estimating process. This subjectivity is illustrated with the estimated amount of opium that is lost during the production process. For many countries, no estimate is offered. For some countries, like Thailand, a constant 10-percent factor is applied; for others, a variable factor is applied. For instance, Burma's loss factor ranges from 8.9 to 12.3 percent. The rationale behind these loss factors is not apparent, and the factors appear to be somewhat arbitrary.

---

[13]The "data on eradication, seizures, labs destroyed, and arrests reflect official GOB (Government of Burma) statistics . . . ," INCSR, 1992, p. 259.

[14]The Burmese "government's political and military accommodations with various ethnic insurgent and trafficking groups, such as the Wa and Kokang, apparently preclude any GOB security/military actions against poppy cultivation, heroin production, and narcotics trafficking in the areas under the groups' control." See INCSR, 1992, p. 36.

Table 2.2

A Comparison of Opium Production Estimates for 1989

	Burma	Laos	Thailand	Mexico	Afghanistan	Iran	Pakistan	Lebanon
NNICC	2,175–3,075	300–460	40–58	85	460–710	200–400	110–150	35–50
INCSR	2,430	210–310	50	66	585	200	130	45
DEA	n.a.	n.a.	n.a.	n.a.	700–800	n.a.	n.a.	n.a.

NOTE: All numbers represent metric tons. The DEA citation can be found in *The NNICC Report*, 1989, p. 49.

This general uncertainty is evident in the opium production estimates illustrated in Table 2.2. The NNICC offers a wide range of values, with the typical high estimate around 50 percent higher than the low NNICC estimate. Moreover, even within the NNICC there are disagreements, such as that over the data for Afghanistan in 1989. The official NNICC estimate on opium production is 460 to 710 metric tons, but DEA, the lead agency within the NNICC, estimates 700 to 800 metric tons. Amidst this apparent uncertainty, the INCSR estimate is frequently between the NNICC's high and low estimates.

There are also revisions from year to year in opium production estimates. For example, the 1989 INCSR reports Laotian opium production in 1988 and 1989 as 210 to 300 metric tons for both years (with no estimate of hectares). However, in the 1992 INCSR, the opium production estimates for 1988 and 1989 are 361 and 375 metric tons, respectively (with hectares [ha] in production reported to be 40,400 and 42,130). Likewise, a range of 23 to 33 metric tons is offered by the INCSR in 1989 for Thailand's 1988 production. The 1992 INCSR report indicates that Thailand's 1988 production was 28 metric tons—the average of the earlier range. Sometimes these differences are explained in terms of newer data or information. For example, the 1992 INCSR states that a study done in Thailand from December 1991 to February 1992 revealed that Thai opium yield is 28 percent lower than previously believed (11.6 kg/ha versus 16 kg/ha) and that the same might be true of Burma's opium production. This also occurred in 1989, when Pakistan's yield was revised upward from 150 to 205 metric tons in light of new data, but sometimes changes are made with no explanation.[15]

This discussion has highlighted many inconsistencies and uncertainties associated with basic factors of the heroin system. Under these circumstances, fundamental estimates, such as the amount produced, the amount consumed in country, the quantity lost during production, or the amount shipped to the United States, are suspect.

---

[15]See Reuter and Ronfeldt (1992) for a discussion of changes in the estimates of Mexican opium production.

3. Overview of the System Description

RAND has developed a series of computer-based spreadsheets to model the heroin production process described in the previous section. We label these spreadsheets, in the aggregate, a system description, and this section provides a general overview. The system description consists of four related spreadsheets, which together can serve both as a database and an analytical tool. We designed flexibility into the system description so analysts can easily substitute data or modify assumptions while preserving the integrity of the system.

Components of the System Description

While the specifics of the drug industries can vary, each industry follows the same overall pattern, which provides the basis of our system description. Figure 3.1 describes the pattern and compares it with our system description components.

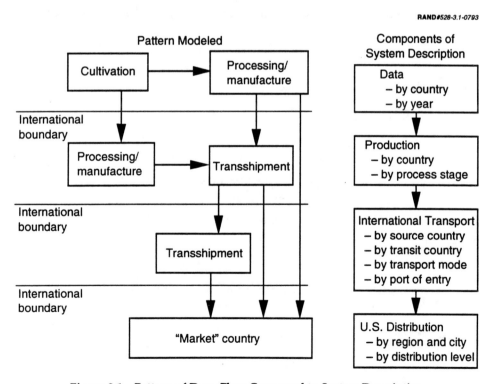

Figure 3.1—Pattern of Drug Flow Compared to System Description

The various activities or functions can be characterized as production, international transportation, and domestic distribution. For convenience, each of these activities has a separate spreadsheet devoted to it.

Four computer-based spreadsheets form the system description for heroin.[1] The first is a **database**, primarily of production-related data (from 1985 to 1991) that is linked to the spreadsheets and can provide the initial conditions.[2] Each record of the database provides data on a country's low and high values for a variety of production estimates. These data are taken from the open literature, primarily the INCSR and the NNICC reports.

Three system spreadsheets mirror the categories of activities noted above: **Production**, **International Transportation**, and **U.S. Distribution**. These spreadsheets model the flow of heroin through the entire system for one year at a time; an extract from the database spreadsheet can provide the initial conditions for a given year, or the analyst can substitute others. The diagram on the right side of Figure 3.1 provides a schematic of the spreadsheet structure.

In spite of the data uncertainties we have discussed, we have tried to create a very comprehensive system framework, primarily because different users may have access to and confidence in data about different parts of the system, and to allow for as comprehensive accounting as possible. It is not necessary to supply data for every parameter in the model. (Appendix C provides more detail for the user.)

Production Spreadsheet

The production spreadsheet begins with an estimate of cultivated area and ends with an estimate of the amount of heroin ready for shipment to the world's markets. It builds an estimate of heroin production using parameters for each stage in the heroin manufacturing process and for each participating (or source) country.[3] Losses due to seizures, consumption, or any other reason are accounted for, as well as transfers of intermediate products between processing countries.

---

[1] The software is Microsoft Excel, and the model can be made available for either PC or Macintosh hardware.

[2] The examples in this section are based on 1991 data.

[3] Conversion parameters mostly depend on where the opium is grown, since this is largely what determines its chemical composition. For this reason, the model keeps an account of where the intermediate product originated.

Embedded graphs show the gross and net production for each producer country at each stage of the manufacturing process. Figure 3.2 is an example of a summary graph that displays each country's "market share" for each stage of the production process. For example, Burma produces most of the world's opium but ships much of it to neighboring Thailand and Laos to be processed into heroin and exported to the world's markets. Meanwhile, Pakistan, with an estimated 1.08 million heroin addicts, has the bulk of the processed heroin.[4]

International Transportation Spreadsheet

The international transportation spreadsheet covers a larger part of the system than any of the other spreadsheets. It takes the amount of heroin ready for export from the production spreadsheet and generates an estimate of the amount successfully smuggled into the United States according to user-determined

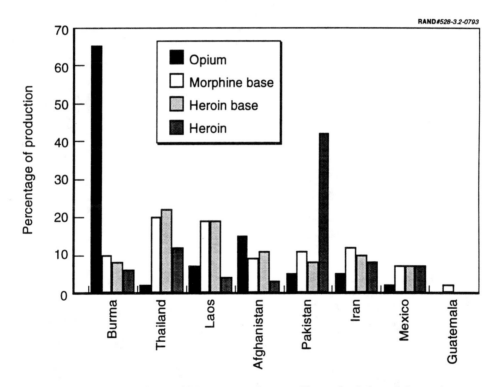

Figure 3.2—Processing and Movement: Country Shares for Selected Countries

---

[4]See *INCSR*, 1992, p. 248. By comparison, Burma is estimated to have 34,000 opium addicts and 12,000 heroin addicts (p. 257), and Thailand is estimated to have up to 132,000 heroin addicts (p. 305). Another estimate places Thailand's heroin addicts at 100,000 to 150,000 (U.S. Congress, House of Representatives, 1989, p. 99).

transshipment parameters. It comprises four different matrices that systematically divide the volume of heroin from producer to transit countries, and then subdivide into other matrices that allocate the heroin to the world's markets,[5] and then to U.S. regions by transportation mode. Moreover, there is the capability to remove heroin from the system either because of foreign seizures or domestic seizures at the point of entry into the United States. Again, built-in graphs, such as Figure 3.3, provide a variety of summary information.

One matrix takes the drug from the producer countries and distributes it to the shipping countries. For example, much of the heroin produced in Southeast Asia is shipped through Thailand and Malaysia. Four different transshipment matrices in the heroin international transportation spreadsheet allow the user to transfer the world's estimated heroin production from country to country. A second matrix takes the drug from the shipping countries and distributes it to the world's markets, including the United States. After foreign seizures are removed from the system, a third matrix is provided that allows the user to distribute the drug among the United States entry regions.

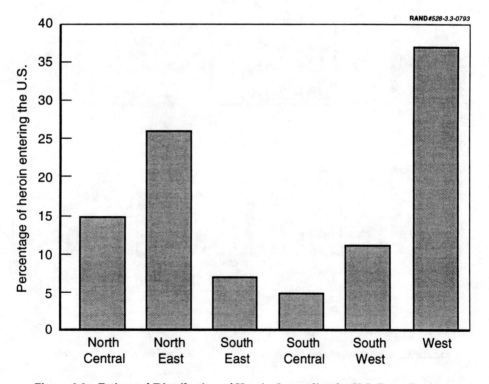

Figure 3.3—Estimated Distribution of Heroin Smuggling by U.S. Entry Region

---

[5]We have included storage as a "market" from which product can be made available for a later year.

At this point in the system description, the United States has been divided into six regions (see Appendix A for a list of the states in each region). The sources of heroin vary among the regions, as do the primary transportation modes. Another matrix defines the drug flow by transportation modes: private or commercial land, sea, or air. Thus, the spreadsheet shows, for example, that in 1991, the West is estimated to have received much of its heroin from commercial sea, while the Northeast gets most of its heroin via commercial air. The final matrix operating in this spreadsheet accounts for those drugs seized at the U.S. borders.

At various points in the system, the analyst can compare model outputs with exogenously produced estimates in which the analyst may have higher confidence. For example, the model keeps a running tabulation of the source of the United States' heroin, and so it is possible to determine the relative percentages received from Southeast Asia, Southwest Asia, and Mexico. This information can, in turn, be compared with estimates like the DEA's Heroin Signature Program data or estimates of the relative percentage of the world illicit *opiate* (opium, morphine, and heroin) consumption between the world's markets.[6] To assist with these comparisons, the model produces estimates from the production spreadsheet and the international transportation spreadsheet in a separate summary spreadsheet.[7]

U.S. Distribution Spreadsheet

The final spreadsheet tracks the domestic distribution of drugs. It begins with the amount successfully smuggled into each of the U.S. entry regions and ends with an estimate of the total number of users in the United States. As with all of the spreadsheets, the analyst can substitute other estimates. A matrix is provided so the user can make interregional transfers and subtract losses—owing either to domestic law enforcement or other removals or inventory losses. Then, depending on what the analyst determines to be typical consumption and purity levels, an estimate is generated of the number of users. This estimate can then be compared to the estimate from the National Household Survey on Drug Abuse, allowing the analyst to calibrate the model in yet another fashion.

---

[6]See ONDCP (1992). The estimated breakdown, which is open to debate, has Asia/Pacific consuming 72 percent, Europe 18 percent, United States 6 percent, and 4 percent to other regions/countries.

[7]The percentages are presented in a summary spreadsheet, which really represents a fifth model spreadsheet. However, there are no data input requirements for this spreadsheet; it simply consolidates into one screen selected information from the other spreadsheets for convenience.

Limitations

The system description's limitations fall into two categories. First, the system description is analytic: It is a description and takes behavior as given. Second, it rests on incomplete and often questionable data. Of course, this same weakness makes the systems approach useful, and indeed, necessary.

From an analytic perspective, the framework is not adaptive. By itself, it cannot provide information on how the system might respond to policy choices or strategies. For instance, suppose an analyst is interested in what impact a 50 percent reduction in Burma's opium production would have on the level of heroin entering the United States. The analyst can simply cut Burma's opium production in half and see how much is entering the United States. However, this assumes that Burmese (and other) traffickers behave similarly regardless of the level of production, when it is quite likely that they behave differently. If the analyst assumes that, for example, 5 percent of Burma's opiates are shipped to the United States, it is not necessarily the case that 5 percent of the crop will be shipped to the United States after production has been reduced by 50 percent. It is perhaps just as likely that markets closer to home (and hence easier to supply) will be supplied first and more distant markets (e.g., Canada and the United States) second. So, the percentage shipped to the United States probably *interacts* with Burma's total production. By itself, the model does not take into account these possible interactions. Instead, it is the responsibility of the user to be cognizant of them. However, the model can incorporate findings from economic and/or behavioral models of particular sectors and show a first approximation of the systemwide effect of policies directed at those sectors.

Also, the framework generally models drug flows in only one direction—from production through consumption. This means if an analyst overrides the data in, for example, the international transportation spreadsheet, the model will show the downstream implications of the analyst's estimates (i.e., the amount entering the United States and distributed in the United States) but will not automatically show the upstream changes in production or processing estimates required to be consistent with the analyst's data. However, these types of problems can be explored by using Excel's Goalseeker or Solver function, allowing the user to derive upstream estimates that would be consistent with changes in downstream data, albeit at a more aggregate level of detail.

Finally, the model does not currently incorporate precursor chemicals as raw materials, although this could be derived exogenously by the analyst. It also estimates only domestic labor in the U.S. Distribution spreadsheet; it does not estimate labor in the other stages of the system. Again, it is certainly possible to add labor as an input for other sectors.

4. Applications for the System Description

The system description has at least three distinct, but related, uses: improving the estimation process, sensitivity analysis, and planning and assessment.

Improving Estimation

The inconsistency of production and consumption estimates has become a serious issue for policymakers. Basic disagreements about whether the drug problem is improving or deteriorating would be at least partially resolved if it were possible to link indicators from different parts of the system. The system description forces consistency, which is not to be confused with accuracy or validity, on the estimation process.

The difficulty of determining the amount of heroin entering the United States is aggravated by the fact that, ostensibly, only a small percentage of the world's production is consumed in the United States.[1] Most estimates of annual U.S. heroin consumption reside in the range of 6 to 9 metric tons,[2] but some have suggested higher numbers.[3] The estimate derived from the model described in this report, which is based on our best efforts to interpret the available data, is 7.8 metric tons. However, it is quite possible that the actual number is substantially higher. For example, assuming the Heroin Signature Program percentages of regional source are generally correct (with Mexican heroin constituting 21 percent of the U.S. market), and the Mexican (and Guatemalan) production is 5.2 metric tons (with all of it shipped to the United States), this then implies that approximately 25 metric tons are shipped to the United States. Obviously, 25 metric tons is significantly higher than 6 to 9 metric tons.

This example illustrates how the model can be used to help evaluate such issues by substituting an alternative estimate and then evaluating the new estimate in

---

[1]One published estimate has the United States consuming 6 percent of the world's *opiates*. See ONDCP (1992).

[2]See, for example, Surrett (1988) and ONDCP (1991), pp. 15–16.

[3]In an interview in June 1992, an ONDCP official indicated that his unofficial guess was between 20 and 30 metric tons. Also, see Hamill and Cooley, (1990). They estimate that there are close to one million heroin addicts in the United States. Some believe that 9 metric tons of heroin are inadequate to meet the demand of this many addicts.

terms of its perturbation of the system.[4] For example, if the current value of 7.8 metric tons is substituted with 25 metric tons, the estimated number of users increases from 686,000 to 2,321,000—a rather large number compared to the frequently cited estimates of 500,000 to 1 million users. If we have high confidence in this range, what other changes would we have to make to arrive within that range of the number of users and still accept the 25–metric ton figure? If we increase average annual consumption from 0.039 kg annually to 0.073 kg annually (an increase of 103 percent),[5] the estimated number of users falls to 1,141,000, which approaches the high end of that range. Increasing average purity levels by 50 percent, from 30 percent pure to 45 percent pure (which is a huge increase, considering that the average purity on the national level was about 27 percent in 1991)[6] decreases the estimated number of users to 761,000 users—nearer the frequently cited 500,000 to 1,000,000 range. Figure 4.1 reflects these changes. The analyst must decide if these changes are substantively acceptable. If these changes are difficult to support, either individually or cumulatively, then it is problematic to accept the 25–metric ton estimate. Conversely, accepting a higher estimate of the number of users requires less dramatic changes in other parameters. The analyst must decide which parameters he or she has the highest confidence in and with which other parameters must be consistent.

---

[4]We are not suggesting that any particular estimate is more correct than any other. We are advocating an analytical structure for imposing a consistency on various system estimates. We offer the example of the Heroin Signature Program because its percentages suggest that an extremely high quantity of heroin is being imported into the United States.

[5]The 1992 *INCSR* estimates that heroin addicts in Thailand consume 0.2 g daily, which is 0.073 kg annually. This estimate was generated by Thailand's Office of Narcotics Control Board (ONCB). In Abt Associates (1991), it is estimated that 33 mg are consumed per day (if 6 metric tons are consumed by 500,000 users), which is 0.012 kg annually. Discussions with a DEA agent reveal that many heavy users can consume between 60 and 90 mg per day, which is about 0.033 kg annually. Except for the Thai estimate, the other numbers are consistent with the estimates drawn up in the early 1980s by the Client Oriented Data Acquisition Process (CODAP). Three classes of users are identified—small, medium, and large—and their average daily consumption of heroin is estimated to be 10 mg, 28 mg, and 87 mg per day, respectively. When weighted by NIDA's estimate of the percentage of the user population in each category, this results in an average consumption level of about 40 mg per day (about 0.015 kg annually). See National Narcotics Intelligence Consumers Committee (1981), p. 99. The average of the Thai estimate (0.012), the DEA agent estimate (0.033), and the Abt Associates estimate (0.012) is 0.0393 kilograms per year. If the weighted CODAP estimate (0.015) is factored into this, the average decreases to 0.0333 per year. The model is currently set at 0.039, but the user can change this to another value.

[6]In 1991, 560 "exhibits" were analyzed by the DEA in its Domestic Monitor Program (DMP). The purity of these exhibits averaged 26.6 percent, with a low of 0.7 percent and a high of 95.6 percent. See *Domestic Monitor Program: An Annual Report on the Source Areas, Cost, and Purity of Retail-Level Heroin, 1991*, U.S. Department of Justice, Drug Enforcement Administration, Office of Intelligence, July 1992. The DMP is a retail-level heroin purchase program designed to provide federal, state, and local law enforcement with intelligence on heroin purity, price, and geographic source areas. The DMP normally collects heroin samples in major metropolitan areas: Atlanta, Boston, Chicago, Dallas, Denver, Detroit, Houston, Los Angeles, Miami, Newark, New Orleans, New York, Philadelphia, Phoenix, San Diego, San Francisco, Seattle, St. Louis, and Washington, D.C.

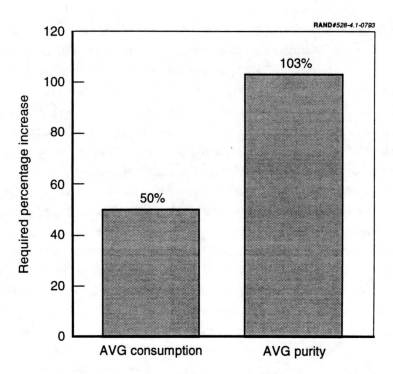

Figure 4.1—Accommodating 25 Metric Tons of Heroin: Required Changes to Selected Parameters

Sensitivity Analysis

Given the limitations of available data, one of the most important contributions of the model, aside from imposing a logical or conditional framework on disparate sources of information, is the ability to analyze parameter sensitivity easily. For instance, Table 4.1 illustrates the percentage change in the three output measures for a 50-percent increase in selected parameter values.

Even from this limited analysis, one can see that changes in some parameters have a much greater impact on the system than changes in other parameters. This information can be useful for, among other things, allocating intelligence resources. Seeing, for example, that the estimated number of users in the United States is increased by over 70 percent when the parameter for Burmese metric tons of opium per hectare is changed by 50 percent highlights the importance of getting this estimate correct. By comparison, Laotian opium consumption and foreign seizures have a comparatively small impact on the outcome measures.

Analytic resources need to be allocated where they will produce the greatest returns. Resources might be focused on the most uncertain parameters that sensitivity analysis has shown to be critical in the determination of the flow of

Table 4.1

Sample Parameter Sensitivity Analysis

Parameters Increased	Gross Supply of Heroin[a]	Heroin Sent to the U.S.[a]	Estimated Number of Users[a]
Opium per hectare (metric tons)			
Burma	78.1	51.1	71.1
Afghanistan	18.7	10.1	13.0
Mexico	1.4	21.3	28.6
Eradication area (hectares)			
Burma	–0.5	–0.3	–0.4
Afghanistan	0.0	0.0	0.0
Mexico	–2.4	–37.0	–48.3
Laos opium consumption (metric tons)	–4.0	–1.8	–2.3
Foreign seizures	n.a.	–4.4	–5.7
U.S. border seizures	n.a.	n.a.	–15.3
Drug purity	n.a.	n.a.	–33.3
Annual consumption	n.a.	n.a.	–33.5

[a]Percentage change for a 50-percent increase in parameter value.

heroin to the United States, although it is also essential to consider the cost of attaining a given percentage reduction in the parameter uncertainty.

Furthermore, to ensure that resources are allocated in a cost-effective fashion, it would be useful to compare current resource allocations with the results of a sensitivity analysis similar to the illustrative analysis in Table 4.1. If inordinate resources are being spent on determining the "correct" value of a parameter that a sensitivity analysis has shown to be relatively unimportant, an alternative allocation could be justified.

Planning and Assessment

A number of programmatic and analytic purposes can be served by tracking regional flows. For instance, this can help the analyst pay attention to the consequences of an increase or decrease in production on the flows of traffic along different routes. For example, Figure 4.2 shows the estimated percentage increase in commercial air drug flow by region when both the Burma and Mexico opium (metric tons) per hectare parameters are increased by 25 percent. One can see radically different implications for planning and assessment depending upon changes (25 percent) in production estimates, and the implications are different depending upon the producing country. Of course, this example assumes that only the production estimate, and not the distribution pattern, is changed.

28

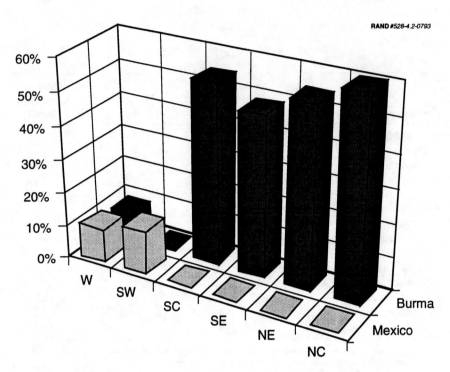

Figure 4.2—Estimated Percentage Increase in Drug Flow by Commercial Air When Opium (Metric Tons) per Hectare Is Increased by 25 Percent

However, one could also easily examine the implications of a change in distribution pattern on the average number of aircraft, boats, or vehicles needed to smuggle drugs into the "new" region of choice.

The system also keeps a running total of which countries (and therefore which regions of the world) are supplying the United States with heroin. The model's current estimate of supply by region contrasts sharply with the reported percentages from the DEA's Heroin Signature Program. The model's regional percentages for U.S. heroin suppliers are 36.1 percent from Southeast Asia, 9.9 percent from Southwest Asia, and 54 percent from Mexico. The HSP estimates suggest very different percentages—58 percent for Southeast Asia, 21 percent for Southwest Asia and 21 percent for Mexico.

Many policymakers have noted the increased production of opium and heroin in Southeast Asia and that region's increasing share of the U.S. market, as measured by the HSP. Most of the SEA heroin is likely entering through the Northeast region of the United States, while most of the Mexican heroin enters through the western regions. If planning is currently predicated on the assumption that most heroin in the United States is from SEA, it is probable that most resources devoted to stemming the flow of heroin are concentrated in the Northeast. However, if, as the model suggests, more heroin is coming from Mexico, more heroin might be entering through the western regions. Therefore, more enforcement resources should be allocated to those regions.

Finally, this framework may serve as a useful tool for better integration of strategic intelligence estimates between law enforcement agencies and the military, or at least for facilitating a dialogue. The military has a long history of gathering and using long-term, strategic intelligence and has a much greater technical collection and fusion capacity than does domestic law enforcement. There is a natural tension between the more short-term and reactive enforcement agencies and the strategically oriented military. The system description may help the two sides develop a common strategic focus and language of criminal methods and infrastructure.

5. Conclusions

The United States has committed substantial resources to stemming the flow of illegal drugs into the United States, yet considerable uncertainty surrounds the basic outlines of the heroin (and other drug) system. This situation is understandable, given that the production and trafficking of narcotics are usually conducted in secrecy. This also makes it extremely difficult to evaluate the accuracy of basic factors regarding the heroin trade. Nevertheless, if policymakers, law enforcement agencies, and analysts are to promulgate, execute, and evaluate effective responses to the drug problem, the basic outlines of the drug system need to be understood more fully.

The model described in this report has at least three distinct, but related, uses that can facilitate a more informed response to the heroin trade. First, it can be used to improve the estimation process. Many estimates are published in the public domain with little or no substantive explanation of how they are derived. This exacerbates the problem of evaluating the accuracy of many basic estimates on the heroin system. This model, however, can be used to evaluate these estimates by examining their perturbation on the system and asking whether these perturbations are sensible. This technique can be especially effective if the analyst has relatively high certainty about some estimates that can be used as "constraints" on the system. Second, the model can be used to perform sensitivity analysis. Since there is uncertainty about many of the estimates, knowing which have the greatest impact on the system can help guide the allocation of intelligence and analytic resources aimed at reducing uncertainty. Third, the model can be a tool for more effective planning and assessment. It can help planners think in terms of a strategic framework, by linking assumptions on production in Southeast Asia to heroin flows in the United States.

Appendix
A. U.S. Region Definitions

The U.S. regions below are used by drug control agencies in tracking the movement and concentration of drugs. Table A.1 shows the regional compositions.

Table A.1

Regional Definitions

NORTHEAST	SOUTH CENTRAL	NORTH CENTRAL
Connecticut	Alabama	Colorado
Delaware	Arkansas	Idaho
Maine	Louisiana	Illinois
Massachusetts	Mississippi	Indiana
Maryland	Tennessee	Iowa
New Hampshire		Kansas
New Jersey	SOUTHWEST	Kentucky
New York	Arizona	Michigan
Pennsylvania	New Mexico	Minnesota
Rhode Island	Oklahoma	Missouri
Vermont	Texas	Montana
		Nebraska
SOUTHEAST	WEST	North Dakota
District of Colombia	California	Ohio
Florida	Nevada	South Dakota
Georgia	Oregon	Utah
North Carolina	Washington	Wisconsin
South Carolina		Wyoming
Puerto Rico		
Virgin Islands		
Virginia		
West Virginia		

32

B. For the User: More Detail About the Spreadsheet System

The Spreadsheets

A schematic of the spreadsheet organization is shown in Figure B.1, where the linkages are denoted by lines. Because the data are sparse, the database spreadsheets represented with shaded lines do not exist; they are nonetheless included in the figure for conceptual accuracy. The data contained in these spreadsheets come primarily from the *International Narcotics Control Strategy Report* (INCSR), the *National Narcotics Intelligence Consumers Committee Report* (NNICC), DEA reports, congressional hearings, and other publicly available sources. The production-related database contains data over several years, but the system spreadsheets model the quantities and flows of drug for one year at a

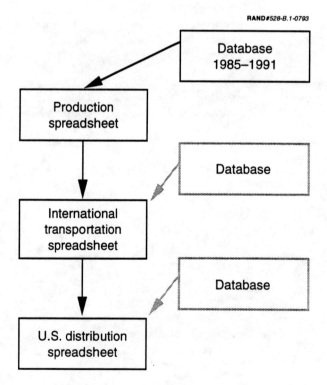

RAND#528-B.1-0793

Figure B.1—Spreadsheet Schematic

time. After describing the spreadsheets in greater detail, this appendix provides some general guidelines for using the model.

Database Spreadsheet

The first spreadsheet is the database and is the starting point for the model; it provides the initial conditions for the production spreadsheet. The user can also substitute his or her own data. This spreadsheet, schematically displayed in Figure B.2, includes a glossary of terms, the database, a "criteria" range and a "data extract" range, which is linked to the next spreadsheet.[1]

Each record in the database is a specific combination of country, year, source reference, and reference low or high value. Table B.1 shows a selection of observations. Column A contains the country, column B the year, and column C the source reference.[2] For each observation, over 25 data elements (fields) can be tracked. Table B.2 shows the list of data elements and their definitions reproduced from the glossary in the database spreadsheet.

RAND #528-B.2-0793

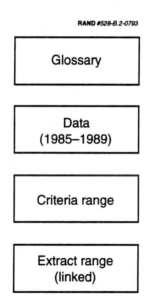

Figure B.2—Database Spreadsheet Outline

---

[1]These are spreadsheet terms. The criteria range is where the user defines what data he or she wants to extract from the database; for instance, all observations for Mexico from 1985–1991. The extract range is where the subset of data defined in the criteria range is displayed.

[2]The source reference numbers are coded to specific reports identified on the spreadsheet. Sources that are used in a more limited way are included in the other spreadsheets as notes behind the relevant data cell(s).

Table B.1

Notional Observation Format

A	B	C	
Country	Year	Reference	
Burma	1991	[2]	Low
Burma	1991	[2]	High
Thailand	1991	[2]	Low
Thailand	1991	[2]	High
Laos	1991	[2]	Low
Laos	1991	[2]	High

NOTE: Bracketed figures [] refer to specific source, e.g., INCSR.

The last two areas in the database spreadsheet are devoted to defining and extracting data from the database for use either in the system spreadsheets or for summary statistics.[3] These areas are partially reproduced in Table B.3. The criteria range is where the user enters the desired characteristics of observations to be extracted. In our example, we have requested observations for 1991 and the low value for reference 2 (which is the INCSR, March 1992). By using the Excel data extract command, observations that meet the criteria are then placed in the data extract range. It is the extract range that is linked to the **Production** spreadsheet. This is the form of the criteria request that should be used if the user wants the extracted data to be used by the system spreadsheets, although any combination of year and reference may be used. Otherwise, if the user wants to use the database exclusively, many creative combinations of criteria can be applied.

Production Spreadsheet

The first system spreadsheet is the production spreadsheet. This spreadsheet begins with the cultivation of the necessary raw material and works through each of the intermediate products, where applicable. It also tracks interregional transfers of intermediate product. The production spreadsheet concludes with the amount of heroin that is ready for export to various markets. Data are presented on

- hectares of opium cultivated
- productivity factors
- loss factors (including consumption, in-country seizures, and other losses)
- intermediate product transportation routes and quantities.

---

[3]A database can provide an analyst with summary statistics about the data. For instance, the DAVERAGE function can be used to find the average cultivation area for all the observations in the database.

Table B.2

Cultivation and Conversion Factors: Heroin

Glossary Variable Name	Units of Measure	Explanation
OPIUMYIELDMT	metric tons/hectare	Amount of raw opium (in mt) per cultivated hectare
OPIUMYIELDKg	kg/hectare	Amount of raw opium (in kg) per cultivated hectare
RO_2_MB	kg raw opium/1 kg morphine base	Raw opium to morphine base conversion factor
MB_2_HB	kg morphine base/ 1 kg heroin base	Morphine base to heroin base conversion factor
HB_2_Heroin	kg heroin base/ 1 kg heroin	Heroin base to heroin conversion factor
RO_2_Heroin	kg raw opium/ 1 kg heroin	Raw opium to heroin conversion factor
CULTIVAREA	hectares	Cultivation area
ERADAREA	hectares	Eradication area
NETCULTIVAREA	hectares	Net cultivation area (after eradication)
OPIUMHARVEST	metric tons	(Cultivation minus eradication) times yield
OPIUMCONSUMD	metric tons	Opium consumed in country
OPIUMSEIZD	metric tons	Opium seized in country
OPIUMLOST	metric tons	Other opium losses in country
OPIUMEXPORTED	metric tons	Opium exported
NETOPIUM	metric tons	Opium harvest minus the three loss categories
GROSSMB	metric tons	NETOPIUM/RO_2_MB
MBCONSUMD	metric tons	Morphine base consumed in country
MBSEIZD	metric tons	Morphine base seized in country
MBLOST	metric tons	Other morphine base losses in country
NETMB	metric tons	Gross morphine base minus the three loss categories
GROSSHB	metric tons	NETMB/MB_2_HB
HBCONSUMD	metric tons	Heroin base consumed in country
HBSEIZD	metric tons	Heroin base seized in country
HBLOST	metric tons	Other heroin base losses in country
NETHB	metric tons	Gross heroin base minus the three loss categories
GROSSHEROIN	metric tons	NETHB/HB_2_HEROIN
HEROINCONSUMD	metric tons	Heroin consumed in country
HEROINLOST	metric tons	Other heroin losses in country
HEROINXPORT	metric tons	Heroin available for export

Table B.3

Database Criteria and Extract Range

CRITERIA

COUNTRY	YEAR	REFERENCE	OPIUMYIELDMT	OPIUMYIELDKg	RO_2_MB	MB_2_HB	HB_2_HEROIN
	1991	[2]LOW	XXXX				

EXTRACT RANGE

COUNTRY	YEAR	REFERENCE	OPIUMYIELDMT	OPIUMYIELDKg	RO_2_MB	MB_2_HB	HB_2_HEROIN
BURMA	1991	[2]LOW	0.0147	14.7	10.7	1	1
THAILAND	1991	[2]LOW	0.0117	11.7	#DIV/0!	1	1
LAOS	1991	[2]LOW	0.0089	8.9	9.8	1	1
AFGHANISTAN	1991	[2]LOW	0.0332	33.2	#DIV/0!	1	1
PAKISTAN	1991	[2]LOW	0.0219	21.9	10.0	1	1
IRAN	1991	[2]LOW	#DIV/0!	#DIV/0!	#DIV/0!	1	1
MEXICO	1991	[2]LOW	0.0109	10.9	10.0	1	1
GUATEMALA	1991	[2]LOW	0.0150	15.0	#DIV/0!	1	1
LEBANON	1991	[2]LOW	0.0100	10.0	5.2	1	1

NOTE: Where you see "#DIV/0!", data are not available, and these numbers could not be calculated. Users can input their own factors in the **Production** spreadsheet.

The general procedure followed in this spreadsheet is to calculate the gross intermediate product, subtract losses, transfer the intermediate product, then process it to the next stage (or intermediate product).[4] Almost all data elements in this spreadsheet are linked to the previous **Database** spreadsheet. However, they can be easily overridden if alternative data are available.

Table B.4 is a representation of the spreadsheet for the initial calculation—harvested area. It begins with cultivated areas for the principal opium producers,[5] subtracts losses due to eradication or other reasons (e.g., fields left fallow), and yields the harvested area. Factors for opium yields per hectare then appear, and the multiplication takes us to the second stage—opium. In this illustration of 1991 data, Burma cultivated an estimated 161,012 hectares of opium in 1991 and a small percentage, about one-half of 1 percent, was eradicated (1,012). On average, in 1991, one hectare yielded 15 kg (or 0.015 metric tons) of opium, so about 2,350 metric tons of opium were available for further processing. Looking to the next stage, we see that this is the amount with which Burma begins.

Table B.4

Production Spreadsheet: First Stage—Cultivation/Production

	CULTIVATED HECTARES BEFORE LOSSES	ERAD AREA	OTHER LOSS	CULTIVATED HECTARES AFTER LOSSES	OPIUM YIELD FACTORS
					(Calculated)
BURMA	161,012	1,012	0	160,000	0.015
THAILAND	4,200	1,200	0	3,000	0.012
LAOS	29,625	0	0	29,625	0.009
AFGHANISTAN	17,190	0	0	17,190	0.033
PAKISTAN	8,645	440	0	8,205	0.022
IRAN	0	0	0	0	#DIV/0!
MEXICO	10,310	6,545	0	3,765	0.011
GUATEMALA	1,721	576	0	1,145	0.015
LEBANON	3,400	0	0	3,400	0.010
TOTAL	236,103	9,773	0	226,330	

[4]The implicit assumption is that the losses are of in-country produced goods.

[5]Note that Colombia is not yet included in the model. This is because opium cultivation in Colombia is a recent phenomenon. An analyst can remedy this, as a short-term solution, by combining, for example, Guatemala and Mexican estimates, and then adding Colombia's data to the positions previously occupied by Guatemala.

As can be seen in Table B.5, Burma has a calculated gross opium supply of 2,350 metric tons.[6] At this point, losses from in-country consumption, seizures, or other (e.g., spoilage, inventory shrinkage) are subtracted from gross opium yield. The fourth column is provided to allow the user to subtract even more than specified in the various published accounts. An additional 900 metric tons of opium were subtracted from the Burmese production, because the INCSR estimate of 150 metric tons was deemed to be insufficient based on interviews with DEA personnel.[7] The net opium yield either is transferred to other countries or remains in the country for further processing.

Figure B.3 illustrates the transfer and conversion of the intermediate product. In this case, the opium is transferred to other countries for processing.

Table B.5

Production Spreadsheet: Second Stage—Opium

(1)			---Minus---				(2)
	Opium Before Losses and Transfers		Opium Consumed	Opium Seized	Opium Other Loss	Additional User Specified Losses	Opium After Losses
	User Deter-mined	Calcu-lated					
BURMA	#N/A	2350.0	150	1.2	278	900	1020.8
THAILAND	#N/A	35.0	29	0.6	5	0	0.4
LAOS	#N/A	265.0	0	0.2	0	120	144.8
AFGHANISTAN	#N/A	570.0	0	0.0	0	425	145.0
PAKISTAN	#N/A	180.0	0	0.0	0	120	60.0
IRAN	200	200.0	0	0.0	0	130	70.0
MEXICO	#N/A	41.0	0	0.1	0	0	40.9
GUATEMALA	#N/A	17.2	0	0.0	0	0	17.2
LEBANON	#N/A	34.0	0	0.0	0	0	34.0
TOTAL		3,692	179	2	283	1,695	1,533

---

[6]Alternatively, the user can determine the amount of opium production and input that amount in the column listed as such. This was done for Iran because there are no published estimates of the cultivated hectares, only gross opium production (200 metric tons).

[7]A "note" is placed behind the Excel cell that explains the justification for the parameter estimate.

TRANSFER TABLE
-OPIUM-

TRANSFER FROM	OPIUM EXPORT	Percentage to allocate?	BURMA	THAILAND	LAOS	AFGHANISTAN	PAKISTAN	IRAN	MEXICO	GUATEMALA	LEBANON	INDIA	MALAYSIA	SYRIA	TURKEY	TOTAL OUTGOING
BURMA	300.0	29.4%		45.0%	25.0%	0.0%	0.0%	0.0%	0.0%	0.0%	0.0%	0.0%	8.0%	0.0%	0.0%	796
THAILAND	0.0	0.0%	0.0%		0.0%	0.0%	0.0%	0.0%	0.0%	0.0%	0.0%	0.0%	0.0%	0.0%	0.0%	0
LAOS	0.0	0.0%	0.0%	0.0%		0.0%	0.0%	0.0%	0.0%	0.0%	0.0%	0.0%	0.0%	0.0%	0.0%	0
AFGHANISTAN	0.0	0.0%	0.0%	0.0%	0.0%		25.0%	25.0%	0.0%	0.0%	0.0%	0.0%	0.0%	0.0%	0.0%	72
PAKISTAN	0.0	0.0%	0.0%	0.0%	0.0%	0.0%		0.0%	0.0%	0.0%	0.0%	0.0%	0.0%	0.0%	0.0%	0
IRAN	0.0	0.0%	0.0%	0.0%	0.0%	0.0%	0.0%		0.0%	0.0%	0.0%	0.0%	0.0%	0.0%	10.0%	7
MEXICO	0.0	0.0%	0.0%	0.0%	0.0%	0.0%	0.0%	0.0%		0.0%	0.0%	0.0%	0.0%	0.0%	0.0%	0
GUATEMALA	0.0	0.0%	0.0%	0.0%	0.0%	0.0%	0.0%	0.0%	75.0%		0.0%	0.0%	0.0%	0.0%	0.0%	13
LEBANON	0.0	0.0%	0.0%	0.0%	0.0%	0.0%	0.0%	0.0%	0.0%	0.0%		0.0%	0.0%	50.0%	0.0%	17
TOTAL INCOMING			0	459	255	0	36	36	13	0	0	0	82	17	7	906 TOTAL OUT / 906 TOTAL IN

(3)

OPIUM AFTER LOSSES AND TRANSFERS	
BURMA	225
THAILAND	460
LAOS	400
AFGHANISTAN	72
PAKISTAN	96
IRAN	99
MEXICO	54
GUATEMALA	4
LEBANON	17
INDIA	0
MALAYSIA	82
SYRIA	17
TURKEY	7
TOTAL	1,533

OPIUM TO MORPHINE BASE CONVERSION FACTORS

	Calculated	User Determined
BURMA	10.7	#N/A
THAILAND	#DIV/0!	10
LAOS	9.8	#N/A
AFGHANISTAN	#DIV/0!	10
PAKISTAN	10.0	#N/A
IRAN	#DIV/0!	10
MEXICO	10.0	#N/A
GUATEMALA	#DIV/0!	10
LEBANON	5.2	#N/A
INDIA	...	10
MALAYSIA	...	10
SYRIA	...	10
TURKEY	...	10

SOURCE DISTRIBUTION

	Burma	Thailand	Laos	Afghanistan	Pakistan	Iran	Mexico	Guatemala	Lebanon	SUM	Non-Pooled Conversion Factor	Pooled Conversion Factor
Burma	100.0%	0.0%	0.0%	0.0%	0.0%	0.0%	0.0%	0.0%	0.0%	100.0%	10.7	10.7
Thailand	99.9%	0.1%	0.0%	0.0%	0.0%	0.0%	0.0%	0.0%	0.0%	100.0%	10.0	10.7
Laos	63.8%	0.0%	36.2%	0.0%	0.0%	0.0%	0.0%	0.0%	0.0%	100.0%	9.8	10.4
Afghanistan	0.0%	0.0%	0.0%	100.0%	0.0%	0.0%	0.0%	0.0%	0.0%	100.0%	10.0	10.0
Pakistan	0.0%	0.0%	0.0%	37.7%	62.3%	0.0%	0.0%	0.0%	0.0%	100.0%	10.0	10.0
Iran	0.0%	0.0%	0.0%	36.5%	0.0%	63.5%	0.0%	0.0%	0.0%	100.0%	10.0	10.0
Mexico	0.0%	0.0%	0.0%	0.0%	0.0%	0.0%	76.0%	24.0%	0.0%	100.0%	10.0	10.0
Guatemala	0.0%	0.0%	0.0%	0.0%	0.0%	0.0%	0.0%	100.0%	0.0%	100.0%	10.0	10.0
Lebanon	0.0%	0.0%	0.0%	0.0%	0.0%	0.0%	0.0%	0.0%	100.0%	100.0%	5.2	5.2
India	0.0%	0.0%	0.0%	0.0%	0.0%	0.0%	0.0%	0.0%	0.0%	0.0%	0.0	0.0
Malaysia	100.0%	0.0%	0.0%	0.0%	0.0%	0.0%	0.0%	0.0%	0.0%	100.0%	10.0	10.7
Syria	0.0%	0.0%	0.0%	0.0%	0.0%	0.0%	0.0%	0.0%	100.0%	100.0%	10.0	5.2
Turkey	0.0%	0.0%	0.0%	0.0%	0.0%	100.0%	0.0%	0.0%	0.0%	100.0%	10.0	10.0

Figure B.3—Transferring and Converting Intermediate Product

Regarding Burmese opium, 45 percent is shipped to Thailand, 25 percent to Laos, and 8 percent to Malaysia to be processed into morphine base.[8] One can see how the opium is redistributed to countries other than those that produced the opium, with some shipped to India, Malaysia, Syria, and Turkey for further processing. After the opium has been redistributed, Burma now has 225 metric tons of opium instead of nearly 2,400 metric tons. These new totals are reflected under the large matrix labeled OPIUM AFTER LOSSES AND TRANSFERS. This opium is converted to morphine base using the country-specific conversion factors, and the same in-country consumption, seizures, other losses, and transfer, then conversion to the next product is continued.[9] The model keeps a running total of the intermediate or final product's originating-country opium. For example, one can see that of the opium being held by Laos, 63.8 percent was grown in Burma and 36.2 in Laos. Ultimately, at the final stage, we can view the percentage distribution of opium source country for each country's supply of heroin. This is useful for at least two reasons.

First, it is useful for creating "pooled conversion factors" during the intermediate product stages. In effect, since the conversion factor is determined to a large extent by the location of opium cultivation, the model pools the sources of each processing country's opium and adjusts the conversion factor to reflect its proportion of the total. For example, Laos's conversion factor is 9.8, which is 9.8 kg of opium to produce 1 kg of morphine base, and Burma's is 10.7. However, when the opium is converted to morphine base, the model notes that 63.8 percent of Laos's opium was grown in Burma (.638 * 10.7 = 6.83) and 36.2 percent was grown in Laos (.362 * 9.8 = 3.55). It then pools the products of these calculations (6.83 + 3.55) to derive the "pooled conversion factor" used to convert Laos' opium to morphine base, which is 10.4.

The second useful purpose becomes apparent in the next spreadsheet, the international transportation spreadsheet, where an analyst might like to identify the regional source of the U.S. heroin supply. Without this tracking mechanism, it would be nearly impossible for the analyst to disentangle the various sources of heroin after it has been shipped, and shipped again, through the many transshipment matrices as it makes its way to the world's markets.

---

[8]These estimated percentages are based on publicly available sources that discuss the important role played by Thailand and Malaysia as processors of Burmese opium.

[9]There are a total of three sets of matrices like the one pictured in Figure B.3. The first, as shown here, is the transfer and conversion of opium to morphine base. The second sequence has the morphine base being converted to heroin base, and the third has the heroin base transformed into usable heroin.

International Transportation

This spreadsheet begins with final product ready for export from the Production spreadsheet just described and estimates the amount that is successfully smuggled into the United States. Simply, as the schematic in Figure B.4 shows, it is a series of input matrices that systematically divides the drug volume from producer countries, to shipping countries, to markets, to U.S. regions, and finally to U.S. regions and transportation modes. This spreadsheet contains the following estimates:

- The amount transiting each smuggler country

- The amount exported to markets other than the United States

- The amount coming into the United States

- The amount, net of seizures, that makes it into the United States by region and transportation mode.

Table B.6 shows the amount of heroin ready for export to the world's markets, and Table B.7 shows its source distribution (as explained in the section on the

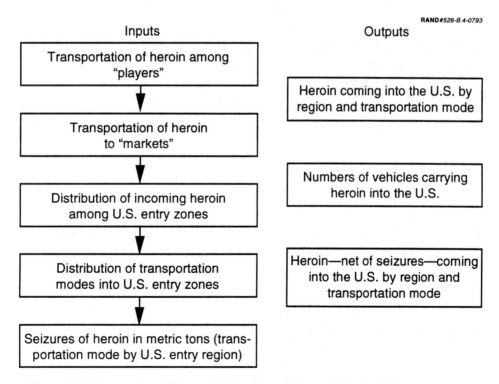

Figure B.4—International Transportation Spreadsheet: A Schematic Representation

Table B.6

Estimate of Heroin Ready for the World's Markets

	Heroin From "HEROPROD" (in metric tons) (1)	Inventory Storage (2)	Alternative Inputs (3)
Burma	10.5	0.0	#N/A
Thailand	4.8	0.0	#N/A
Laos	7.7	0.0	#N/A
Afghanistan	1.8	0.0	#N/A
Pakistan	0.0	0.0	#N/A
Iran	0.6	0.0	#N/A
Mexico	5.5	0.0	#N/A
Guatemala	0.2	0.0	#N/A
Lebanon	1.6	0.0	#N/A
India	0.0	0.0	#N/A
Malaysia	7.7	0.0	#N/A
Syria	4.9	0.0	#N/A
Turkey	4.3	0.0	#N/A
Total	49.5	0.0	#N/A

Production spreadsheet). An estimated 49.5 metric tons of heroin are ready for export to the world's markets.

There are four transshipment matrices, with the first one shown in Table B.8. The four matrices allow the user to transship several times, but only once is necessary for the model.

After the transshipments have occurred, the next matrix (Table 2 in the International Transportation spreadsheet) distributes the drug to the markets. Table B.9 is a representation of this matrix—a sample of shipping countries are listed in the left-hand column and the markets are identified across the top row. The United States and Canada are identified separately; all other markets are denoted by continent. We have included an additional "market"—storage— which can hold the product for distribution in a later year.[10] Below each shipping country listed in the left-hand column is a figure representing the metric tons of heroin ready for shipment to market. The user can enter the percentage of this amount that is distributed to each market, and the computer

---

[10]For simplicity, we have provided one storage point; conceptually, there could be storage at most stages of the production process.

Table B.7
Source Distribution (in percent)

	Burma	Thai.	Laos	Afgh.	Pak.	Iran	Mex.	Guat.	Leb.	Total
Burma	100.0	0.0	0.0	0.0	0.0	0.0	0.0	0.0	0.0	100.0
Thailand	99.9	0.1	0.0	0.0	0.0	0.0	0.0	0.0	0.0	100.0
Laos	63.8	0.0	36.2	0.0	0.0	0.0	0.0	0.0	0.0	100.0
Afghanistan	0.0	0.0	0.0	86.9	13.1	0.0	0.0	0.0	0.0	100.0
Pakistan	0.0	0.0	0.0	0.0	0.0	0.0	0.0	0.0	0.0	0.0
Iran	0.0	0.0	0.0	36.5	0.0	63.5	0.0	0.0	0.0	100.0
Mexico	0.0	0.0	0.0	0.0	0.0	0.0	73.1	26.9	0.0	100.0
Guatemala	0.0	0.0	0.0	0.0	0.0	0.0	0.0	100.0	0.0	100.0
Lebanon	0.0	0.0	0.0	0.0	0.0	0.0	0.0	0.0	100.0	100.0
India	0.0	0.0	0.0	0.0	0.0	0.0	0.0	0.0	0.0	0.0
Malaysia	100.0	0.0	0.0	0.0	0.0	0.0	0.0	0.0	0.0	100.0
Syria	0.0	0.0	0.0	0.0	0.0	0.0	0.0	0.0	100.0	100.0
Turkey	0.0	0.0	0.0	27.0	0.0	73.0	0.0	0.0	0.0	100.0

Table B.8

Transshipment Matrix

(INPUT IN PERCENTS, CONVERTED TO METRIC TONS)

TRANSPORT TO: FROM	BURMA	THAILAND	LAOS	AFGHANISTAN	PAKISTAN	IRAN	MEXICO	GUATEMALA	LEBANON	INDIA	MALAYSIA	SYRIA	TURKEY	HONG KONG	NEPAL	NIGERIA	PHILIPPINES	SINGAPORE	NETHERLANDS	AMOUNT EXPORTED	AMOUNT IMPORTED	AMOUNT REMAINING
BURMA	0.0%	45.0%	10.0%	0.0%	0.0%	0.0%	0.0%	0.0%	0.0%	15.0%	10.0%	0.0%	0.0%	10.0%	0.0%	0.0%	0.0%	10.0%	0.0%	100%		
THAILAND	0.0%																					
LAOS	0.0%	75.0%																				
AFGHANISTAN	0.0%																					
PAKISTAN	0.0%																					
IRAN	0.0%												100.0%									
MEXICO	0.0%						100.0%															
GUATEMALA	0.0%																					
LEBANON	0.0%											75.0%										
INDIA	0.0%																					
MALAYSIA	0.0%																					
SYRIA	0.0%																					
TURKEY	0.0%																					
AMOUNT IMPORTED																						

SUM CHECKS

Table B.9

Shipping Heroin to the World's Markets

FROM:	Canada	S.E. Asia/ Pacific	Europe/ Mid East	To Storage	Unknown Dest.	To Other Market	Amount to U.S.	Alt. Amount to U.S.
MEXICO	0.0%	0.0%	0.0%	0.0%	0.0%	0%	100%	#N/A
5.7	0.0	0.0	0.0	0.0	0.0	0.0	5.7	#N/A
GUATEMALA	0.0%	0.0%	0.0%	0.0%	0.0%	0%	100%	#N/A
0.0	0.0	0.0	0.0	0.0	0.0	0.0	0.0	#N/A
TURKEY	0.0%	0.0%	100.0%	0.0%	0.0%	100%	0%	#N/A
2.5	0.0	0.0	2.5	0.0	0.0	2.5	0.0	#N/A
NIGERIA	0.0%	0.0%	50.0%	0.0%	0.0%	50%	50%	#N/A
5.2	0.0	0.0	2.6	0.0	0.0	2.6	2.6	#N/A
	−	−	−	−	−	−	−	−
TOTALS	1.5	19.4	18.1	0.0	0.0	39.0	10.5	#N/A

	Canada	SEA/ Pacific	EUR/ME	Storage	Unknown	Sub-total	U.S.	Alt. to U.S.
	3.0%	39.3%	36.6%	0.0%	0.0%		21.2%	

will calculate the metric tonnage directly below the input value. For example, according to our calculations for 1991, Mexico had 5.7 metric tons of heroin to smuggle, of which 100 percent was shipped to United States.[11] On the other hand, Nigeria's heroin is distributed equally between the two markets of Europe/Mid-East and the United States.[12] The source or rationale for the 100 percent estimate is included in a note "behind" the cell, and, in this example, is an estimate based on the Drug Enforcement Agency (DEA) smuggling routes map (1989) and the INCSR (1992) and other miscellaneous information.[13] Alternatively, the user can simply input the estimated percentage headed for the U.S. market and ignore the other markets. In either case, this matrix estimates the volume of drug being sent to the United States. The next step is to estimate how much is being smuggled into each region of the United States.

In Table B.10, the user must provide an estimate of the total amount of heroin seized in foreign locations that was destined for the U.S. market. In this example,

---

[11]The source distribution table indicates that of Mexico's 5.7 metric tons of heroin, 70.3 originated in Mexico and 29.7 in Guatemala.

[12]Nigeria's heroin is 78.1 percent Burmese, 10 percent Laotian, 10.3 percent Afghan, 1.5 Pakistani, and only 0.1 percent Thai.

[13]The existence of a note behind a cell is indicated by a small square (arrow on the Macintosh) in the upper right-hand corner of the cell.

Table B.10

Foreign Seizures

10.50	Estimated metric tons headed for the U.S. market **before** foreign seizures.
0.845	Estimated metric tons destined for the U.S. but seized in foreign locations.
8.05%	Of the total that is destined for U.S. but is seized in foreign locations.
9.66	Estimated metric tons headed for the U.S. market **after** foreign seizures.

using illustrative data, about 854 kg (or 0.845 metric tons) seized in foreign locations (normally foreign ports) were deemed to be destined for the United States. Since it is not known where this heroin originated (at least not to RAND), an equal proportion is subtracted from each country's total to remove this amount from the system.

The next input matrix is patterned very similarly to the matrix for distributing the heroin to the world's markets, except in this case the heroin is distributed to the six U.S. regions. The smuggling countries are shown in the left-hand column with the amount destined for the U.S. market, and the regions of the United States are shown across the top row (these regions are defined in Appendix A). The user has the option to enter the percentage that is smuggled from each shipping country to each region of the United States. The routes identified in this spreadsheet were approximated from a DEA map of drug trafficking routes. The absence of an entry indicates that there is no route between the shipping country and the U.S. region.[14]

The next input matrix is again patterned similarly to the previous two matrices (see Table B.11). It distributes the drug flow into each U.S. region among a number of transportation modes:

- Commercial air

- Commercial sea

- Commercial land

- Private air

- Private sea

- Private land.

---

[14]Drug Trafficking Routes, DEA Map, 1989.

Table B.11

Heroin Entering U.S. Regions by Transportation Mode

	North-Central	North-east	South-east	South-Central	South-west	West
Commercial air	100%	100%	100%	50%	39%	27%
Private air	0%	0%	0%	0%	0%	0%
Commercial land	0%	0%	XXX	XXX	0%	0%
Private land	0%	0%	XXX	XXX	61%	1%
Commercial sea	0%	0%	0%	50%	0%	72%
Private sea	0%	0%	0%	0%	0%	0%
Total	100.0%	100.0%	100.0%	100.0%	100.0%	100.0%

Commercial air includes passengers carrying illicit drugs, as well as packaged drugs contained in cargo. Commercial land includes tractor trailers, while private land includes private and recreational vehicles, as well as persons carrying packages. The others are self-explanatory. The distribution of drug traffic into these transportation modes can be based on seizure or other relevant data. For convenience, illustrative default distributions are provided. The distributions are specific to each entry region; that is, every route feeding the Southeast United States will have the same distribution based on the seizures in that region. (Default values can be easily overridden.)

The final input matrix in the **International Transportation** spreadsheet is for estimates of seizures, roughly limited to those at U.S. borders (see Table B.12).

Within the international transportation spreadsheet, and several columns to the right of these input matrices, are tables of results. The first table shows the

Table B.12

Heroin Seizures by Region and Transportation Mode

	North-Central	North-east	South-east	South-Central	South-west	West	Total by Mode
Commercial air	0.201	1.129	0.016	0.000	0.016	0.238	1.5990
Private air	0.000	0.000	0.000	0.000	0.000	0.000	0.0000
Commercial land	0.000	0.000	---	--	0.000	0.000	0.0000
Private land	0.000	0.000	---	---	0.024	0.008	0.0324
Commercial sea	0.000	0.000	0.000	0.000	0.000	0.628	0.6280
Private sea	0.000	0.000	0.000	0.000	0.000	0.000	0.0000
Total	0.201	1.129	0.016	0.000	0.040	0.874	2.259
By region	8.9%	50.0%	0.7%	0.0%	1.8%	38.7%	100%

amount of drug smuggled over the various routes to the United States. Table B.13 shows a section of this table. Each entry in the table represents the estimate of metric tonnage of heroin that traveled from the shipping countries listed in the left-hand column, to the U.S. entry region listed along the top row, sorted by transportation mode. For example, an estimated 1.1 metric tons traveled from Mexico to the West region of the United States by commercial air in 1991.

The same format is repeated for the other transportation modes, and this information, coupled with estimated data on average load sizes, can be used to estimate the number of land, sea, and air vehicles carrying the heroin into the United States. Finally, various summary statistics are offered, and Table B.14 shows some of them.

The analyst can view the consequences and implications of his or her parameters and estimates up to this point in the model. For example, 45.9 percent of all heroin is entering through the West region, followed by 20.3 percent in the Northeast. Planners should ask themselves if this conforms to current planning and assumptions. Also, regarding the issue of totals by source region, does the

Table B.13

Output: Volume of Heroin by Route and Transportation Mode

Commercial Air	North-Central	North-East	South-East	South-Central	South-West	West	Totals
Burma	0.0	0.0	0.0	0.0	0.0	0.0	0.0
Thailand	0.0	0.0	0.0	0.0	0.0	0.0	0.0
Laos	0.0	0.0	0.0	0.0	0.0	0.0	0.0
Afghanistan	0.0	0.0	0.0	0.0	0.0	0.0	0.0
Pakistan	0.0	0.0	0.0	0.0	0.0	0.0	0.1
Iran	0.0	0.0	0.0	0.0	0.0	0.0	0.0
Mexico	0.0	0.0	0.0	0.0	0.5	1.1	1.6
Guatemala	0.0	0.0	0.0	0.0	0.0	0.0	0.0
Lebanon	0.0	0.0	0.0	0.0	0.0	0.0	0.0
India	0.0	0.0	0.0	0.0	0.0	0.0	0.0
Malaysia	0.0	0.0	0.0	0.0	0.0	0.0	0.0
Syria	0.0	0.0	0.0	0.0	0.0	0.0	0.0
Turkey	0.0	0.0	0.0	0.0	0.0	0.0	0.0
Hong Kong	0.2	0.2	0.0	0.0	0.0	0.1	0.5
Nepal	0.0	0.0	0.0	0.0	0.0	0.0	0.0
Nigeria	0.7	1.2	0.2	0.1	0.0	0.0	2.3
Philippines	0.0	0.0	0.0	0.0	0.0	0.0	0.0
Singapore	0.0	0.0	0.0	0.0	0.0	0.0	0.0
Netherlands	0.2	0.5	0.2	0.0	0.0	0.0	0.9

Table B.14

Summary Statistics for Incoming Heroin to the United States

BY REGION:	NC	NE	SE	SC	SW	West
TOTALS	1.2	2.0	0.5	0.3	1.3	4.4
	11.9%	20.3%	4.7%	3.6%	13.5%	45.9%

TOTALS BY TRANSPORT MODE:			SEA	SWA	MEX
AIR:	5.5	56.57%	85.4%	95.0%	30.3%
commercial	5.5	56.57%	85.4%	95.0%	30.3%
private	0.0	0.00%	0.0%	0.0%	0.0%
LAND:	0.8	8.63%	0.1%	0.0%	15.9%
commercial	0.0	0.00%	0.0%	0.0%	0.0%
private	0.8	8.63%	0.1%	0.0%	15.9%
SEA:	3.4	34.80%	14.4%	5.0%	53.9%
commercial	3.4	34.80%	14.4%	5.0%	53.9%
private	0.0	0.00%	0.0%	0.0%	0.0%
			3.5	1.0	5.2

TOTALS BY EXPORT COUNTRY:			TOTALS BY SOURCE COUNTRY:		
Burma	0.0	0.0%	Burma	32.3%	3.1
Thailand	0.0	0.0%	Thailand	0.0%	0.0
Laos	0.0	0.0%	Laos	3.8%	0.4
Afghanistan	0.0	0.0%	Afghanistan	4.7%	0.5
Pakistan	0.1	1.0%	Pakistan	0.6%	0.1
Iran	0.0	0.0%	Iran	1.7%	0.2
Mexico	5.2	54.0%	Mexico	38.0%	3.7
Guatemala	0.0	0.0%	Guatemala	16.0%	1.5
Lebanon	0.0	0.0%	Lebanon	2.9%	0.3
India	0.0	0.0%	TOTAL	100.0%	9.7
Malaysia	0.0	0.0%			
Syria	0.0	0.0%	TOTALS BY SOURCE REGION		
Turkey	0.0	0.0%	SEA	36.1%	3.5
Hong Kong	0.9	8.8%	SWA	9.8%	1.0
Nepal	0.0	0.0%	MEX	54.0%	5.2
Nigeria	2.4	24.9%	TOTAL	100%	9.7
Philippines	0.1	1.0%			
Singapore	0.0	0.0%			
Netherlands	1.0	10.3%			
TOTAL	9.7	100%			

percentage distribution between SEA, SWA, and MEX conform to the widely held belief that SEA is the dominant supplier of heroin to the United States?

U.S. Distribution

The final system spreadsheet (Table B.15) tracks the domestic distribution of heroin. It begins with the amount successfully smuggled into each of the U.S. entry regions. (Again, while these values are linked to the previous spreadsheet, they can be overridden.) A column is available to add domestic production to the amount imported. While this is not necessarily relevant for heroin, it is an important contribution to the estimate of marijuana supply, and we have tried to keep the system descriptions for different drugs as consistent as possible. In the context of heroin, this column could be used for another estimate of storage. This table generates an estimate of the total amount of heroin available for domestic distribution.

The remainder of this spreadsheet distributes the drug throughout the United States and calculates the numbers of individuals in each of the drug-market hierarchy levels, based on estimates of the supply, purity levels, and annual usage. The final table compares the estimated user prevalence with the National Institute of Drug Abuse (NIDA) National Household Survey estimate.[15] There is even less data available for this part of the system description than for the production and international transportation sections, so almost all the numbers shown here are meant to be illustrative.

Table B.15

Incoming Heroin by Region

	Net of POE Seizures	Domestic Production	TOTAL	Alternate TOTAL
North Central	0.95	0.00	0.95	#N/A
Northeast	0.83	0.00	0.83	#N/A
Southeast	0.44	0.00	0.44	#N/A
South Central	0.35	0.00	0.35	#N/A
Southwest	1.26	0.00	1.26	#N/A
West	3.56	0.00	3.56	#N/A
Total	7.40	0.00	7.40	#N/A

[15]*National Household Survey on Drug Abuse: Population Estimates 1988*, U.S. Department of Health and Human Services, National Institute on Drug Abuse, 1989.

Figure B.5 is a schematic of this spreadsheet. Once we have the estimate of the amount of drug entering the various U.S. regions, we provide the capability to estimate interregional transfers to get an estimate of the gross amount ready for sales.

The procedure here mirrors the procedure in the **International Transportation** spreadsheet: The user enters the estimate of the percentage of drug available that is shipped from the entry regions to the demand regions and enters estimates of the losses due either to domestic enforcement or inventory, and other losses. The user then has the option to allocate the regional quantities to cities within the region. The cities included are those identified as high-intensity trafficking areas by the National Drug Control Strategy Report, January 1990, augmented by those classified by the FBI as Level I or II cities for drug trafficking activities. The next two matrices contain inputs for the final table, which in turn calculates the numbers of individuals involved in the trade at each level in the market. These calculations are based on estimates of how much heroin is handled or consumed. The regions and cities appear in the left-hand column, and the trade hierarchy appears across the top. Each entry represents the numbers of individuals involved in the trade for the given year, based on the drug supply. The final

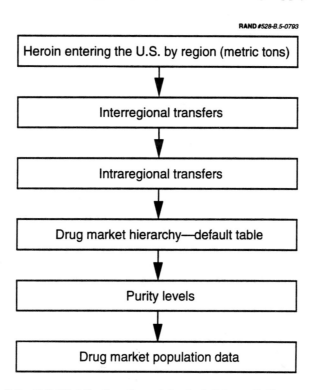

RAND #528-B.5-0793

Heroin entering the U.S. by region (metric tons)

Interregional transfers

Intraregional transfers

Drug market hierarchy—default table

Purity levels

Drug market population data

Figure B.5—U.S. Distribution Spreadsheet: A Schematic Representation

columns compare the drug-user prevalence (based on supply estimates) to a demand-based estimate of drug use to determine whether the two estimates are at all consistent. This final table is reproduced in Table B.16; as one can see, there are an estimated 192,000 users in the Northeast region, which is more or less consistent with most estimates concerning New York City (usually estimates are

Table B.16
Drug Market Population Data

	Estimated Users (in 000s)	Population (in 000s)	Calculated Prevalence	National Household Survey Prevalence	Ratio
North Central					
Chicago (II)	0	0	NA	0.3%	NA
Detroit (II)	0	0	NA	0.3%	NA
All Other	159	58,031	0.3%	0.3%	0.93
North East					
Boston (II)	0	0	NA	0.7%	NA
Newark (II)	0	0	NA	0.7%	NA
New York (I)	0	0	NA	0.7%	NA
All Other	192	47,152	0.4%	0.7%	0.62
South East					
Atlanta	0	0	NA	0.2%	NA
Miami (I)	0	0	NA	0.2%	NA
All Other	21	30,996	0.1%	0.2%	0.34
South Central					
New Orleans	0	0	NA	0.2%	NA
All Other	50	14,860	0.3%	0.2%	1.67
South West					
El Paso (~I)	0	0	NA	0.2%	NA
Houston (I)	0	0	NA	0.2%	NA
All Other	108	19,900	0.5%	0.2%	2.46
West					
Los Angeles (I)	0	0	NA	0.3%	NA
San Diego (II)	0	0	NA	0.3%	NA
San Francisco (II)	0	0	NA	0.3%	NA
Seattle	0	0	NA	0.3%	NA
All Other	156	30,193	0.5%	0.3%	1.73
U.S. Total	686	201,131	0.3%	0.3%	

around 200,000), and an estimated 686,000 nationwide, which is also consistent with most estimates (usually estimates are around 750,000).[16]

Summary Spreadsheet

There is one final spreadsheet, the **Summary Spreadsheet**. This spreadsheet does not require any data input by the user, and the only new information is the percentage distribution to the world markets. This is obtained by combining information on consumption within the producing countries with heroin shipments to the world's markets. In short, for the sake of convenience, this spreadsheet pulls together selected information from the other spreadsheets (see Figure B.6).

Year	1991	
Heroin Ready For Export to the World Market	49.5	metric tons
Percentage Distribution to the World Markets		
Canada	1.0%	
SEA/Pacific	79.8%	
Europe/Middle East	12.1%	
Storage	0.0%	
Unknown/Elsewhere	0.1%	
United States	7.0%	
Amount of Heroin Entering the United States	7.4	metric tons
Source Percentage Distribution of U.S. Heroin		
SEA	36.1%	
SWA	9.8%	
MEX	54.0%	
Estimated Number of Users in the United States	686,326	

Figure B.6—The Summary Spreadsheet

---

[16]One should not interpret this as our definitive estimate of the number of heroin users in the United States. Rather, it should be interpreted as the number of users there must be *if one accepts all previous parameter estimates in the model.*

C. Spreadsheet Guidelines

The system description consists of four speadsheets:

1. HERODATA for heroin database
2. HEROPROD for processing and movement
3. HEROTRAN for international transportation
4. HEROUSA for U.S. distribution

The graphs associated with the worksheets are saved in separate files known as chart files.

Each spreadsheet has cells that are linked to data in the previous worksheet, so all the spreadsheets must be open. The chart files should generally be open as well. Any spreadsheets not of immediate interest can be hidden with the **Window Hide** command. Once the worksheets are all open, they can be saved with the **File Save Workspace** command. A workspace file contains a list of all the documents open at the time the **Save Workspace** command is chosen. So the next time one uses the model, the files can be opened all at once just by clicking on the workspace file.

A spreadsheet that has cells linked to data in another worksheet is "dependent" on that other worksheet. For instance, HEROPROD is dependent on HERODATA, HEROTRAN is dependent on HEROPROD, and so on. As long as all the dependent worksheets are open, if one saves a worksheet under a different name, the linked cell references in the dependent worksheet(s) will also change. If a chart file is open (and not hidden), any changes made in the data it is linked to will be immediately reflected in the graph.

Linked cells use absolute addresses (not relative addresses for the cells they link to). So, let us say one expanded the database in HERODATA, and the data extract range now starts at row 230 rather than row 226. One will get incorrect (if any) data in the linked dependent cells in HEROPROD unless one manually changes the address those cells link to (see the Excel manual). One will also need to redefine the database range in HERODATA using the **Data Set Database** command.

It is good practice to make a working copy of the original "master" files and store the master files in a safe place—perhaps a separate directory (PC) or folder (Mac). It is also good practice to click on the *Read Only* option in the Open

Document dialog box. When this box is checked, the program allows one to view and edit the file, but requires one to save it under another name so one cannot overwrite the file one started with. This feature is especially helpful if one is doing, say, sensitivity analyses and wants to save several versions with different data estimates.

Nomenclature

Blue cells are meant to alert the user that they are linked to other worksheets. Of course, the user may override and enter other data, but to restore these links, he or she will have to use the "master" version (or a knowledgeable user can restore them manually). Red cells indicate that a user should enter his or her own data.

Other cells with a little red square (IBM) or arrow (Apple) in the upper right-hand corner have a note "behind" the cell explaining something about the data in the cell. If there is a column of like numbers, the note may reference the entire column (and may appear behind only the first cell). This note can be viewed by using the command **Formula Note** or by double-clicking on the cell. The dialog box will also show a list of other notes in the spreadsheet that can be viewed by clicking on any entry in the list. The Excel manual describes how to view or print all the notes on a spreadsheet.

Some Features of Using the Database in HERODATA

Users who are unfamiliar with using a spreadsheet database are strongly encouraged to read the Excel manual chapter on analyzing and reporting database information.

The defined criteria range in the master spreadsheet has two rows under the field names. Excel treats criteria entered on the same row as a logical AND, while criteria entered on different rows are treated as a logical OR. In the example in the main text, "1989" is entered under the field name "YEAR," and "[2]LOW" is entered in the same row under the field named "REFERENCE." In extracting records, the program interprets this to mean, "pick those records that have a year of 1989 *and* a reference of [2]LOW." If no criterion is entered under a field name, the program interprets it to mean, "pick any (all) criteria for that field." Thus, if an entire row in the criteria range is left completely blank, the program will extract all records in the database. It is good practice to put stoppers in the form of "XXXX" or the like under a field name in each row in the criteria range to avoid inadvertently extracting all the data records.

In the master spreadsheet, the extract range is at the bottom of the spreadsheet and is defined as the row of field names. This is done to avoid guessing at how much space might be needed to extract records. However, each time one uses the Data Extract command, all previous data in the extract range are cleared. If one wants to save these data for some reason, one should copy them to another area of the worksheet or to another worksheet. A database can provide an analyst with summary statistics about the data. For instance, the DAVERAGE function can be used to find the average cultivation area. See Database Functions in the Excel manual.

Cell Locations

The figures on the following pages depict the various sections of the four spreadsheets. The text across from each figure describes that section of the spreadsheet.

	A	B	C	D	E	F	G	H	I	J	K
1											
2					PROCESSING AND MOVEMENT: HEROIN					PAGE 1	
3					YEAR=	1991					
4	FIRST STAGE - CULTIVATION/PRODUCTION										
5	(In Hectares)										
6											
7	(1)				--MINUS--		(2)				
8	CULTIVATED HECTARES				ERAD.	OTHER	CULTIVATED HECTARES				
9	BEFORE LOSSES				AREA	LOSS	AFTER LOSSES			OPIUM YIELD	
10										FACTORS	
11	BURMA		161,012		1,012	0	160,000			(Calculated)	
12	THAILAND		4,200		1,200	0	3,000			0.0147	
13	LAOS		29,625		0	0	29,625			0.0117	
14	AFGHANISTAN		17,190		0	0	17,190			0.0089	
15	PAKISTAN		8,645		440	0	8,205			0.0332	
16	IRAN		0		0	0	0			0.0219	
17	MEXICO		10,310		6,545	0	3,765			#DIV/0!	
18	GUATEMALA		1,721		576	0	1,145			0.0109	
19	LEBANON		3,400		0	0	3,400			0.0150	
20										0.0100	
21											
22		TOTAL	236,103								
23						TOTAL	226,330				
24											
25											
26	SECOND STAGE -- OPIUM										
27	(In Metric Tons)										
28											
29	(1)				-- MINUS--				(2)		
30	OPIUM BEFORE LOSSES			OPIUM	OPIUM	OPIUM	Additional		OPIUM AFTER		
31	AND TRANSFERS			CONSUMED	SEIZED	OTHERLOSS	User Specified		LOSSES		
32		User Dete	Calculated				Losses				
33	BURMA	#N/A	2350.0	150	1.2	278	900		1020.8		
34	THAILAND	#N/A	35.0	29	0.6	5	0		0.4		
35	LAOS	#N/A	265.0	0	0.2	0	120		144.8		
36	AFGHANISTAN	#N/A	570.0	0	0.0	0	425		145.0		
37	PAKISTAN	#N/A	180.0	0	0.0	0	120		60.0		
38	IRAN	200	200.0	0	0.0	0	130		70.0		
39	MEXICO	#N/A	41.0	0	0.1	0	0		40.9		
40	GUATEMALA	#N/A	17.2	0	0.0	0	0		17.2		
41	LEBANON	#N/A	34.0	0	0.0	0	0		34.0		
42											
43											
44		TOTAL	3,692	179	2	283	1,695	TOTAL	1,533		
45											
46											
47											

Figure C.1—The Cultivation and Production of Opium (Cells A1 to K47)

Figure C.1 shows the first tables in the heroin production spreadsheet, HEROPROD.XLS. Virtually all of the data shown in this figure are linked to the data spreadsheet, HERODATA.XLS. The user can, of course, override any of these values. The user may also input his or her own data, however, in the cell range B33 to B41 (which overrides the calculated figure in the next column) and in the cell range G33 to G41. One can see that Mexico's cultivated hectares before losses value (10,310) is shown in cell C17, eradication area (6,545) in cell E17, and other losses (0) in cell F17. The estimated hectares after losses value (3,765) is shown in G17. The estimated opium yield factor, or the metric tons of opium produced from one hectare (0.0109), is displayed in cell J17. Since Mexico has an estimated 3,765 hectares and a leaf yield factor of 0.0109, the resulting estimated production of opium is 41 metric tons, which is illustrated in cell C39. (The user can input an alternative estimate in B39.) Mexican consumption (0), seizures (0.1), other losses (0), and additional losses are presented in cells D39, E39, F39, and G39, respectively. The resulting estimate of Mexican opium production ready for conversion to morphine base (40.9) is shown in cell I39.

TRANSFER TABLE — OPIUM

TRANSFER TO

TRANSFER FROM	OPIUM EXPORT	Percentage to allocate?	BURMA	THAILAND	LAOS	AFGHANISTAN	PAKISTAN	IRAN	MEXICO	GUATEMALA	LEBANON	INDIA	MALAYSIA	SYRIA	TURKEY	TOTAL OUTGOING
BURMA	300.0	29.4%		45.0%	25.0%	0.0%	0.0%	0.0%	0.0%	0.0%	0.0%	0.0%	8.0%	0.0%	0.0%	796
THAILAND	0.0	0.0%	0.0%		0.0%	0.0%	0.0%	0.0%	0.0%	0.0%	0.0%	0.0%	0.0%	0.0%	0.0%	0
LAOS	0.0	0.0%	0.0%	0.0%		0.0%	0.0%	0.0%	0.0%	0.0%	0.0%	0.0%	0.0%	0.0%	0.0%	0
AFGHANISTAN	0.0	0.0%	0.0%	0.0%	0.0%		25.0%	25.0%	0.0%	0.0%	0.0%	0.0%	0.0%	0.0%	0.0%	72
PAKISTAN	0.0	0.0%	0.0%	0.0%	0.0%	0.0%		0.0%	0.0%	0.0%	0.0%	0.0%	0.0%	0.0%	0.0%	0
IRAN	0.0	0.0%	0.0%	0.0%	0.0%	0.0%	0.0%		0.0%	0.0%	0.0%	0.0%	0.0%	0.0%	10.0%	7
MEXICO	0.0	0.0%	0.0%	0.0%	0.0%	0.0%	0.0%	0.0%		0.0%	0.0%	0.0%	0.0%	0.0%	0.0%	0
GUATEMALA	0.0	0.0%	0.0%	0.0%	0.0%	0.0%	0.0%	0.0%	75.0%		0.0%	0.0%	0.0%	0.0%	0.0%	13
LEBANON	0.0	0.0%	0.0%	0.0%	0.0%	0.0%	0.0%	0.0%	0.0%	0.0%		0.0%	0.0%	50.0%	0.0%	17
TOTAL INCOMING			0	459	255	0	36	36	13	0	0	0	82	17	7	

TOTAL OUT 906
TOTAL IN 906

(3) OPIUM AFTER LOSSES AND TRANSFERS

	OPIUM AFTER LOSSES AND TRANSFERS
BURMA	225
THAILAND	460
LAOS	400
AFGHANISTAN	72
PAKISTAN	96
IRAN	99
MEXICO	54
GUATEMALA	4
LEBANON	17
INDIA	0
MALAYSIA	82
SYRIA	17
TURKEY	7
TOTAL	**1,533**

OPIUM TO MORPHINE BASE CONVERSION FACTORS

	Calculated	User Determined
BURMA	10.7	#N/A
THAILAND	#DIV/0!	10
LAOS	9.8	#N/A
AFGHANISTAN	#DIV/0!	10
PAKISTAN	10.0	#N/A
IRAN	#DIV/0!	10
MEXICO	#DIV/0!	10
GUATEMALA	10.0	#N/A
LEBANON	5.2	#N/A
INDIA	....	10
MALAYSIA	....	10
SYRIA	....	10
TURKEY	....	10

SOURCE DISTRIBUTION

	Burma	Thailand	Laos	Afghanistan	Pakistan	Iran	Mexico	Guatemala	Lebanon	SUM	Non-Pooled Conversion Factor	Pooled Conversion Factor
Burma	100.0%	0.0%	0.0%	0.0%	0.0%	0.0%	0.0%	0.0%	0.0%	100.0%	10.7	10.7
Thailand	99.9%	0.1%	0.0%	0.0%	0.0%	0.0%	0.0%	0.0%	0.0%	100.0%	10.0	10.7
Laos	63.8%	0.0%	36.2%	0.0%	0.0%	0.0%	0.0%	0.0%	0.0%	100.0%	9.8	10.4
Afghanistan	0.0%	0.0%	0.0%	100.0%	0.0%	0.0%	0.0%	0.0%	0.0%	100.0%	10.0	10.0
Pakistan	0.0%	0.0%	0.0%	37.7%	62.3%	0.0%	0.0%	0.0%	0.0%	100.0%	10.0	10.0
Iran	0.0%	0.0%	0.0%	36.5%	0.0%	63.5%	0.0%	0.0%	0.0%	100.0%	10.0	10.0
Mexico	0.0%	0.0%	0.0%	0.0%	0.0%	0.0%	76.0%	24.0%	0.0%	100.0%	10.0	10.0
Guatemala	0.0%	0.0%	0.0%	0.0%	0.0%	0.0%	0.0%	100.0%	0.0%	100.0%	10.0	10.0
Lebanon	0.0%	0.0%	0.0%	0.0%	0.0%	0.0%	0.0%	0.0%	100.0%	100.0%	5.2	5.2
India	0.0%	0.0%	0.0%	0.0%	0.0%	0.0%	0.0%	0.0%	0.0%	0.0%	10.0	0.0
Malaysia	100.0%	0.0%	0.0%	0.0%	0.0%	0.0%	0.0%	0.0%	0.0%	100.0%	10.0	10.7
Syria	0.0%	0.0%	0.0%	0.0%	0.0%	0.0%	0.0%	0.0%	100.0%	100.0%	10.0	5.2
Turkey	0.0%	0.0%	0.0%	0.0%	0.0%	100.0%	0.0%	0.0%	0.0%	100.0%	10.0	10.0

Figure C.2—Transferring and Converting Intermediate Product (Cells A46 to W93)

Figure C.2 shows the next section of the heroin production spreadsheet, HEROPROD.XLS. The user may decide whether to ship opium from one country to another (it could be shipped to another country for consumption, storage, or further processing). The percentage to be shipped should be entered in the cell range D53 to P69. For example, Burma is shipping 45 percent of its opium to Thailand, as reflected in cell E53. As a guide for the amount to ship, the numbers in columns B53 to C69 are prelinked from the data spreadsheet. Once the transshipments have occurred, the amount of opium after losses and transfers is shown in cells D77 to D89. The next step entails converting the opium to morphine base, and the conversion factors are found in cells G77 to H89. In some cases, these conversion factors can be calculated, but in others, the user must supply them.[1] Finally, the source distribution matrix in cells K75 to U89 indicates the source of the opium for each country's supply. For instance, 76 percent of Mexico's 54 metric tons was grown in Mexico, and 24 percent was grown in Guatemala. The pooled conversion factor takes these percentages into account when calculating the value of the opium to morphine base conversion factor.

---

[1]This is because insufficient data are available in the INCSR and NNICC documents to derive the conversion factors. Consequently, those data must come from another source, although the model currently has estimated values for these factors.

	A	B	C	D	E	F	G	H	I	J
94	============	=======	==========	=========	========	===========	============	========	===========	========
95										
96	THIRD STAGE - MORPHINE BASE (No. 1 Heroin)									
97	(In Metric Tons)									
98										
99	(1)								(2)	
100	MORPHINE BASE BEFORE LOSSES					-- MINUS--			MORPHINE BASE AFTER	
101	AND TRANSFERS			CONSUMED	SEIZED	OTHERLOSS	User Specified		LOSSES	
102							Losses			
103	BURMA		21.0	0	0	0	0		21.0	
104	THAILAND		43.1	0	0	0	0		43.1	
105	LAOS		38.6	0	0	0	0		38.6	
106	AFGHANISTAN		7.2	0	0	0	0		7.2	
107	PAKISTAN		9.6	0	0	0	0		9.6	
108	IRAN		9.9	0	0	0	0		9.9	
109	MEXICO		5.4	0	0	0	0		5.4	
110	GUATEMALA		0.4	0	0	0	0		0.4	
111	LEBANON		3.3	0	0	0	0		3.3	
112	INDIA		0.0	0	0	0	0		0.0	
113	MALAYSIA		7.7	0	0	0	0		7.7	
114	SYRIA		3.3	0	0	0	0		3.3	
115	TURKEY		0.7	0	0	0	0		0.7	
116										
117										
118		TOTAL	150.2					TOTAL	150.2	
119										
120										

Figure C.3—Producing Morphine Base (Cells A94 to J120)

Figure C.3 shows the next section of the heroin production spreadsheet, HEROPROD.XLS. The user can input data on the amount of morphine base that is consumed, seized, or lost in the range of cells D103 to G115. Mexico's value is 5.4 (cell C109). This is derived by taking its estimated amount of opium, which is 54 metric tons (cell D83), and dividing it by its pooled conversion factor, which is 10 (cell W83). Since no morphine base is subtracted, Mexico emerges with 5.4 metric tons (cell I109).

64

TRANSFER TABLE — MORPHINE BASE

TRANSFER FROM \ TRANSFER TO	BURMA	THAILAND	LAOS	AFGHANISTAN	PAKISTAN	IRAN	MEXICO	GUATEMALA	LEBANON	INDIA	MALAYSIA	SYRIA	TURKEY	TOTAL OUTGOING
BURMA		20.0%	0.0%	0.0%	0.0%	0.0%	0.0%	0.0%	0.0%	0.0%	0.0%	0.0%	0.0%	4.21
THAILAND	0.0%		0.0%	0.0%	0.0%	0.0%	0.0%	0.0%	0.0%	0.0%	0.0%	0.0%	0.0%	0.00
LAOS	0.0%	0.0%		0.0%	0.0%	0.0%	0.0%	0.0%	0.0%	0.0%	0.0%	0.0%	0.0%	0.00
AFGHANISTAN	0.0%	0.0%	0.0%		0.0%	0.0%	0.0%	0.0%	0.0%	0.0%	0.0%	0.0%	0.0%	0.00
PAKISTAN	0.0%	0.0%	0.0%	20.0%		0.0%	0.0%	0.0%	0.0%	0.0%	0.0%	0.0%	0.0%	1.93
IRAN	0.0%	0.0%	0.0%	0.0%	0.0%		0.0%	0.0%	0.0%	0.0%	0.0%	0.0%	20.0%	1.99
MEXICO	0.0%	0.0%	0.0%	0.0%	0.0%	0.0%		0.0%	0.0%	0.0%	0.0%	0.0%	0.0%	0.00
GUATEMALA	0.0%	0.0%	0.0%	0.0%	0.0%	0.0%	50.0%		0.0%	0.0%	0.0%	0.0%	0.0%	0.22
LEBANON	0.0%	0.0%	0.0%	0.0%	0.0%	0.0%	0.0%	0.0%		0.0%	0.0%	50.0%	0.0%	1.63
INDIA	0.0%	0.0%	0.0%	0.0%	0.0%	0.0%	0.0%	0.0%	0.0%		0.0%	0.0%	0.0%	0.00
MALAYSIA	0.0%	0.0%	0.0%	0.0%	0.0%	0.0%	0.0%	0.0%	0.0%	0.0%		0.0%	0.0%	0.00
SYRIA	0.0%	0.0%	0.0%	0.0%	0.0%	0.0%	0.0%	0.0%	0.0%	0.0%	0.0%		0.0%	0.00
TURKEY	0.0%	0.0%	0.0%	0.0%	0.0%	0.0%	0.0%	0.0%	0.0%	0.0%	0.0%	0.0%		0.00
TOTAL INCOMING	0.0	4.2	0.0	1.9	0.0	0.0	0.2	0.0	0.0	0.0	0.0	1.6	2.0	10.0 TOTAL OUT
														10.0 TOTAL IN

(3)

MORPHINE BASE AFTER LOSSES AND TRANSFERS

BURMA	16.8
THAILAND	47.3
LAOS	38.6
AFGHANISTAN	9.2
PAKISTAN	7.7
IRAN	7.9
MEXICO	5.6
GUATEMALA	0.2
LEBANON	1.6
INDIA	0.0
MALAYSIA	7.7
SYRIA	4.9
TURKEY	2.7
TOTAL	150.2

MORPHINE BASE TO HEROIN BASE CONVERSION FACTORS

	Calculated	User Determined
Burma	1.0	#N/A
Thailand	1.0	#N/A
Laos	1.0	#N/A
Afghanistan	1.0	#N/A
Pakistan	1.0	#N/A
Iran	1.0	#N/A
Mexico	1.0	#N/A
Guatemala	1.0	#N/A
Lebanon	1.0	#N/A
India		1
Malaysia		1
Syria		1
Turkey		1

SOURCE DISTRIBUTION

	Burma	Thailand	Laos	Afghanistan	Pakistan	Iran	Mexico	Guatemala	Lebanon	SUM	Non-Pooled Conversion Factor	Pooled Conversion Factor
Burma	100.0%	0.0%	0.0%	0.0%	0.0%	0.0%	0.0%	0.0%	0.0%	100.0%	1.0	1.0
Thailand	99.9%	0.1%	0.0%	0.0%	0.0%	0.0%	0.0%	0.0%	0.0%	100.0%	1.0	1.0
Laos	63.8%	0.0%	36.2%	0.0%	0.0%	0.0%	0.0%	0.0%	0.0%	100.0%	1.0	1.0
Afghanistan	0.0%	0.0%	0.0%	86.9%	13.1%	0.0%	0.0%	0.0%	0.0%	100.0%	1.0	1.0
Pakistan	0.0%	0.0%	0.0%	37.7%	62.3%	0.0%	0.0%	0.0%	0.0%	100.0%	1.0	1.0
Iran	0.0%	0.0%	0.0%	36.5%	0.0%	63.5%	0.0%	0.0%	0.0%	100.0%	1.0	1.0
Mexico	0.0%	0.0%	0.0%	0.0%	0.0%	0.0%	73.1%	26.9%	0.0%	100.0%	1.0	1.0
Guatemala	0.0%	0.0%	0.0%	0.0%	0.0%	0.0%	0.0%	100.0%	0.0%	100.0%	1.0	1.0
Lebanon	0.0%	0.0%	0.0%	0.0%	0.0%	0.0%	0.0%	0.0%	100.0%	100.0%	1.0	1.0
India	0.0%	0.0%	0.0%	0.0%	0.0%	0.0%	0.0%	0.0%	0.0%	0.0%	0.0	1.0
Malaysia	100.0%	0.0%	0.0%	0.0%	0.0%	0.0%	0.0%	0.0%	0.0%	100.0%	1.0	1.0
Syria	0.0%	0.0%	0.0%	0.0%	0.0%	0.0%	0.0%	0.0%	100.0%	100.0%	1.0	1.0
Turkey	0.0%	0.0%	0.0%	27.0%	0.0%	73.0%	0.0%	0.0%	0.0%	100.0%	1.0	1.0

Figure C.4—Transferring Morphine Base and Its Conversion to Heroin Base (Cells A121 to W172)

Figure C.4 shows the next section of the heroin production spreadsheet, HEROPROD.XLS. The user may decide whether to ship morphine base from one country to another (it could be shipped to another country for consumption, shortage, or further processing). The percentage to be shipped should be entered in the cell range C126 to O150. For example, Burma is shipping 20 percent of its morphine base to Thailand, as reflected in cell D126. Once the transshipments have occurred, the amount of morphine base after losses and transfers is shown in cells D157 to D169. The next step entails converting the morphine base to heroin base, and the conversion factors are found in cells G157 to H169. In some cases, these conversion factors can be calculated, but in others, the user must supply them. Finally, the source distribution matrix in cells K155 to U169 indicates the source of the morphine base for each country's supply. For instance, 73.1 percent of Mexico's 5.6 metric tons was grown in Mexico and 26.9 percent was grown in Guatemala. The pooled conversion factor takes these percentages into account when calculating the value of the opium to morphine base conversion factor.

	A	B	C	D	E	F	G	H	I	J
173	========	=======	==========	=========	========	===========	============	========	===========	========
174										
175	FOURTH STAGE -- HEROIN BASE (No. 2 Heroin)									
176	(In Metric Tons)									
177	(1)								(2)	
178	BASE BEFORE LOSSES				-- MINUS--				BASE AFTER	
179	AND TRANSFERS			CONSUMED	SEIZED	OTHERLOSS	User Specified		LOSSES	
180							Losses			
181	BURMA		16.8	0	0	0	0		16.8	
182	THAILAND		47.3	0	0	0	0		47.3	
183	LAOS		38.6	0	0	0	0		38.6	
184	AFGHANISTAN		9.2	0	0	0	0		9.2	
185	PAKISTAN		7.7	0	0	0	0		7.7	
186	IRAN		7.9	0	0	0	0		7.9	
187	MEXICO		5.6	0	0	0	0		5.6	
188	GUATEMALA		0.2	0	0	0	0		0.2	
189	LEBANON		1.6	0	0	0	0		1.6	
190	INDIA		0.0	0	0	0	0		0.0	
191	MALAYSIA		7.7	0	0	0	0		7.7	
192	SYRIA		4.9	0	0	0	0		4.9	
193	TURKEY		2.7	0	0	0	0		2.7	
194										
195										
196		TOTAL	150.2					TOTAL	150.2	
197										

Figure C.5—Producing Heroin Base (Cells A173 to J197)

Figure C.5 shows the next section of the heroin production spreadsheet, HEROPROD.XLS. The user can input data on the amount of heroin base that is consumed, seized, or lost in the range of cells D181 to G193. Mexico's value is 5.6 (cell C187). This is derived by taking its estimated amount of morphine base, which is 5.6 metric tons (cell D163), and dividing it by its pooled conversion factor, which is 1 (cell W163). Since no heroin base is subtracted, Mexico emerges with 5.6 metric tons (cell I187).

TRANSFER TABLE
--HEROIN BASE:

TRANSFER TO

TRANSFER FROM	BURMA	THAILAND	LAOS	AFGHANISTAN	PAKISTAN	IRAN	MEXICO	GUATEMAL	LEBANON	INDIA	MALAYSIA	SYRIA	TURKEY	TOTAL OUTGOING
BURMA		10.0%	0.0%	0.0%	0.0%	0.0%	0.0%	0.0%	0.0%	0.0%	0.0%	0.0%	0.0%	1.68
THAILAND	0.0%		0.0%	0.0%	50.0%	0.0%	0.0%	0.0%	0.0%	0.0%	0.0%	0.0%	0.0%	23.65
LAOS	0.0%	0.0%		0.0%	80.0%		0.0%	0.0%	0.0%	0.0%	0.0%	0.0%	0.0%	30.89
AFGHANISTAN	0.0%	0.0%	0.0%		80.0%	0.0%	0.0%	0.0%	0.0%	0.0%	0.0%	0.0%	0.0%	7.34
PAKISTAN	0.0%	0.0%	0.0%	0.0%		0.0%	0.0%	0.0%	0.0%	0.0%	0.0%	0.0%	0.0%	0.00
IRAN	0.0%	0.0%	0.0%	0.0%		0.0%		0.0%	0.0%	0.0%	0.0%	0.0%	20.0%	1.59
MEXICO	0.0%	0.0%	0.0%	0.0%	0.0%	0.0%		0.0%	0.0%	0.0%	0.0%	0.0%	0.0%	0.00
GUATEMALA	0.0%	0.0%	0.0%	0.0%	0.0%	0.0%	0.0%		0.0%	0.0%	0.0%	0.0%	0.0%	0.00
LEBANON	0.0%	0.0%	0.0%	0.0%	0.0%	0.0%	0.0%	0.0%		0.0%	0.0%	0.0%	0.0%	0.00
INDIA	0.0%	0.0%	0.0%	0.0%	0.0%	0.0%	0.0%	0.0%	0.0%		0.0%	0.0%	0.0%	0.00
MALAYSIA	0.0%	0.0%	0.0%	0.0%	0.0%	0.0%	0.0%	0.0%	0.0%	0.0%		0.0%	0.0%	0.00
SYRIA	0.0%	0.0%	0.0%	0.0%	0.0%	0.0%	0.0%	0.0%	0.0%		0.0%		0.0%	0.00
TURKEY	0.0%	0.0%	0.0%	0.0%	0.0%	0.0%	0.0%	0.0%	0.0%	0.0%	0.0%	0.0%		0.00
TOTAL INCOMING	0.0	1.7	0.0	0.0	61.9	0.0	0.0	0.0	0.0	0.0	0.0	0.0	1.6	65.2 TOTAL OUT

65.2 TOTAL IN

HEROIN BASE AFTER LOSSES AND TRANSFERS — **CONVERSION FACTORS** — **SOURCE DISTRIBUTION**

	Heroin Base	Calculated	User Determined	Burma	Thailand	Laos	Afghanistan	Pakistan	Iran	Mexico	Guatemala	Lebanon	SUM	Non-Pooled Conversion Factor	Pooled Conversion Factor
Burma	15.2	1.0	#N/A	100.0%	0.0%	0.0%	0.0%	0.0%	0.0%	0.0%	0.0%	0.0%	100.00%	1.0	1.0
Thailand	25.3	1.0	#N/A	99.9%	0.1%	0.0%	0.0%	0.0%	0.0%	0.0%	0.0%	0.0%	100.00%	1.0	1.0
Laos	7.7	1.0	#N/A	63.8%	0.0%	36.2%	0.0%	0.0%	0.0%	0.0%	0.0%	0.0%	100.00%	1.0	1.0
Afghanistan	1.8	1.0	#N/A	0.0%	0.0%	0.0%	86.9%	13.1%	0.0%	0.0%	0.0%	0.0%	100.00%	1.0	1.0
Pakistan	69.6	1.0	#N/A	62.3%	0.0%	16.1%	13.3%	8.3%	0.0%	0.0%	0.0%	0.0%	100.00%	1.0	1.0
Iran	6.4	1.0	#N/A	0.0%	0.0%	0.0%	36.5%	0.0%	63.5%	0.0%	0.0%	0.0%	100.00%	1.0	1.0
Mexico	5.6	1.0	#N/A	0.0%	0.0%	0.0%	0.0%	0.0%	0.0%	73.1%	26.9%	0.0%	100.00%	1.0	1.0
Guatemala	0.2	1.0	#N/A	0.0%	0.0%	0.0%	0.0%	0.0%	0.0%	0.0%	100.0%	0.0%	100.00%	1.0	1.0
Lebanon	1.6	1.0	#N/A	0.0%	0.0%	0.0%	0.0%	0.0%	0.0%	0.0%	0.0%	100.0%	100.00%	1.0	1.0
India	0.0		1	100.0%	0.0%	0.0%	0.0%	0.0%	0.0%	0.0%	0.0%	0.0%	0.00%	0.0	0.0
Malaysia	7.7		1	0.0%	0.0%	0.0%	0.0%	0.0%	0.0%	0.0%	0.0%	0.0%	100.00%	1.0	1.0
Syria	4.9		1	0.0%	0.0%	0.0%	0.0%	0.0%	0.0%	0.0%	0.0%	100.0%	100.00%	1.0	1.0
Turkey	4.3		1	0.0%	0.0%	0.0%	30.5%	0.0%	69.5%	0.0%	0.0%	0.0%	100.00%	1.0	1.0
TOTAL	150.2														

Figure C.6—Transferring Heroin Base and Converting It to Heroin (Cells A198 to W250)

Figure C.6 shows the next section of the heroin production spreadsheet, HEROPROD.XLS. The user must decide whether to ship heroin base from one country to another (it could be shipped to another country for consumption, storage, or further processing). The percentage to be shipped should be entered in the cell range C204 to O228. For example, Burma is shipping 10 percent of its morphine base to Thailand, as reflected in cell D204. Once the transshipments have occurred, the amount of morphine base after losses and transfers is shown in cells D234 to D246. The next step entails converting the heroin base to heroin, and the conversion factors are found in cells G234 to H246. In some cases, these conversion factors can be calculated, but in others, the user must supply them. Finally, the source distribution matrix in cells K232 to U246 indicates the source of the heroin base for each country's supply. The pooled conversion factor takes these percentages into account when calculating the value of the heroin base to heroin conversion factor.

	A	B	C	D	E	F	G	H	I	J
✏										
251	===========	=======	==========	=========	========	===========	============	========	===========	========
252										
253	FINAL STAGE – HEROIN (No. 3 & No. 4 Heroin)									
254	(In Metric Tons)									
255	(1)								(2)	
256	HEROIN BEFORE LOSSES				-- MINUS--				HEROIN READY	
257				CONSUMED	SEIZED	OTHERLOSS	User Specified		FOR EXPORT	
258							Losses			
259	BURMA		15.2	4.5	0.1	0.0	0.0		10.5	
260	THAILAND		25.3	4.5	1.7	0.0	14.3		4.8	
261	LAOS		7.7	0.0	0.0	0.0	0.0		7.7	
262	AFGHANISTAN		1.8	0.0	0.0	0.0	0.0		1.8	
263	PAKISTAN		69.6	50.0	6.0	0.0	13.6		0.0	
264	IRAN		6.4	0.0	0.0	0.0	5.7		0.6	
265	MEXICO		5.6	0.0	0.1	0.0	0.0		5.5	
266	GUATEMALA		0.2	0.0	0.0	0.0	0.0		0.2	
267	LEBANON		1.6	0.0	0.0	0.0	0.0		1.6	
268	INDIA		0.0	0	0	0	0.0		0.0	
269	MALAYSIA		7.7	0	0	0	0.0		7.7	
270	SYRIA		4.9	0	0	0	0.0		4.9	
271	TURKEY		4.3	0	0	0	0.0		4.3	
272										
273										
274		TOTAL	150.2	59.0	8.0	0.0	33.6	TOTAL	49.6	
275										
276										
277										

Figure C.7—Producing Heroin (Cells A251 to J277)

Figure C.7 shows the next section of the heroin production spreadsheet, HEROPROD.XLS. The user can input data on the amount of heroin that is consumed, seized, or lost in the range of cells D259 to G271. Burma's value is 15.2 (cell C259). This is derived by taking its estimated amount of heroin base, which is 15.2 metric tons (cell D234), and dividing it by its pooled conversion factor, which is 1 (cell W234). An estimated 4.5 metric tons are consumed (cell D259) and 0.1 (E259) is seized. Consequently, Burma emerges with 10.5 metric tons of heroin (cell I259).

	A	B	C	D	E	F	G	H	I	J	K	L	M	N	O	P
1															SCREEN 1	
2						INTERNATIONAL TRANSPORTATION:					HEROIN					
3							YEAR =		1991							
4			HEROIN													
5			FROM		INVENTORY											
6			"HEROPROD"		FROM		ALTERNATIVE									
7			(IN MTs)		STORAGE		INPUTS									
8			(1)		(2)		(3)									
9	BURMA		10.5		0.0		#N/A		NOTE:							
10	THAILAND		4.8		0.0		#N/A		TABLE 1. USES COL. (1) DATA LINKED TO HEROPROD.XLS							
11	LAOS		7.7		0.0		#N/A		PLUS COL.(2) DATA INPUT BY USER--							
12	AFGHANISTAN		1.8		0.0		#N/A		UNLESS ANY ALTERNATIVE DATA IS ENTERED IN COL. (3).							
13	PAKISTAN		0.0		0.0		#N/A		COL. (2) INPUTS SHOULD BE STORAGE FROM PRIOR YEAR(S).							
14	IRAN		0.6		0.0		#N/A									
15	MEXICO		5.5		0.0		#N/A									
16	GUATEMALA		0.2		0.0		#N/A									
17	LEBANON		1.6		0.0		#N/A									
18	INDIA		0.0		0.0		#N/A									
19	MALAYSIA		7.7		0.0		#N/A									
20	SYRIA		4.9		0.0		#N/A									
21	TURKEY		4.3		0.0		#N/A									
22																
23	TOTAL		49.6		0.0		#N/A									
24																

Figure C.8—International Transportation of Heroin (Cells A1 to P24)

Figure C.8 shows the first section of the heroin transportation spreadsheet, HEROTRAN.XLS. The user decides whether to add more heroin into the system. If so, these data would be added in the range of cells E9 to E21 for "storage" or G9 to G21 for alternative inputs. The source distribution matrix is located in the range of cells AV7 to BF21. The source distribution table indicates where each country's heroin supply was grown.

TABLE 1A. TRANSPORTATION OF HEROIN AMONG "PLAYERS"
(INPUT IN PERCENTS, CONVERTED TO METRIC TONS)

TRANSPORT TO:

FROM	BURMA	THAILAND	LAOS	AFGHANISTAN	PAKISTAN	IRAN	MEXICO	GUATEMALA	LEBANON	INDIA	MALAYSIA	SYRIA	TURKEY	HONG KONG	NEPAL	NIGERIA	PHILIPPINES	SINGAPORE	NETHERLANDS	AMOUNT EXPORTED	AMOUNT IMPORTED	AMOUNT REMAINING
BURMA (10.5)		45.0% 4.7	10.0% 1.1	0.0% 0.0	0.0% 0.0	0.0% 0.0		0.0% 0.0	0.0% 0.0	15.0% 1.6	10.0% 1.1	0.0% 0.0	0.0% 0.0	10.0% 1.1	0.0% 0.0	0.0% 0.0	0.0% 0.0	10.0% 1.1	0.0% 0.0	100% 10.5	0.0	0.0
THAILAND (4.8)	0.0% 0.0		0.0% 0.0	0.0% 0.0	0.0% 0.0	0.0% 0.0		0.0% 0.0	0.0% 0.0	0.0% 0.0	0.0% 0.0	0.0% 0.0	0.0% 0.0	0.0% 0.0	0.0% 0.0	0.0% 0.0	0.0% 0.0	0.0% 0.0	0.0% 0.0	0% 0.0	10.5	15.3
LAOS (7.7)	0.0% 0.0	75.0% 5.8		0.0% 0.0	0.0% 0.0	0.0% 0.0		0.0% 0.0	0.0% 0.0	0.0% 0.0	25.0% 1.9	0.0% 0.0	0.0% 0.0	0.0% 0.0	0.0% 0.0	0.0% 0.0	0.0% 0.0	0.0% 0.0	0.0% 0.0	100% 7.7	1.1	1.1
AFGHANISTAN (1.8)	0.0% 0.0	0.0% 0.0	0.0% 0.0		90.0% 1.7	0.0% 0.0		0.0% 0.0	0.0% 0.0	0.0% 0.0	0.0% 0.0	2.5% 0.1	7.5% 0.1	0.0% 0.0	0.0% 0.0	0.0% 0.0	0.0% 0.0	0.0% 0.0	0.0% 0.0	100% 1.8	0.0	0.0
PAKISTAN (0.0)	0.0% 0.0	0.0% 0.0	0.0% 0.0	0.0% 0.0		0.0% 0.0		0.0% 0.0	0.0% 0.0	0.0% 0.0	0.0% 0.0	0.0% 0.0	0.0% 0.0	0.0% 0.0	0.0% 0.0	0.0% 0.0	0.0% 0.0	0.0% 0.0	0.0% 0.0	0% 0.0	1.7	1.7
IRAN (0.0)	0.0% 0.0	0.0% 0.0	0.0% 0.0	0.0% 0.0	0.0% 0.0			0.0% 0.0	0.0% 0.0	0.0% 0.0	0.0% 0.0	0.0% 0.0	100.0% 0.8	0.0% 0.0	0.0% 0.0	0.0% 0.0	0.0% 0.0	0.0% 0.0	0.0% 0.0	100% 0.8	0.0	0.0
MEXICO (5.5)	0.0% 0.0	0.0% 0.0	0.0% 0.0	0.0% 0.0	0.0% 0.0	0.0% 0.0		0.0% 0.0	0.0% 0.0	0.0% 0.0	0.0% 0.0	0.0% 0.0	0.0% 0.0	0.0% 0.0	0.0% 0.0	0.0% 0.0	0.0% 0.0	0.0% 0.0	0.0% 0.0	0% 0.0	0.2	5.7
GUATEMALA (0.2)	0.0% 0.0	0.0% 0.0	0.0% 0.0	0.0% 0.0	0.0% 0.0	0.0% 0.0	100.0% 0.2		0.0% 0.0	0.0% 0.0	0.0% 0.0	0.0% 0.0	0.0% 0.0	0.0% 0.0	0.0% 0.0	0.0% 0.0	0.0% 0.0	0.0% 0.0	0.0% 0.0	100% 0.2	0.0	0.0
LEBANON (1.6)	0.0% 0.0	0.0% 0.0	0.0% 0.0	0.0% 0.0	0.0% 0.0	0.0% 0.0		0.0% 0.0		0.0% 0.0	0.0% 0.0	75.0% 1.2	0.0% 0.0	0.0% 0.0	0.0% 0.0	0.0% 0.0	0.0% 0.0	0.0% 0.0	0.0% 0.0	75% 1.2	0.0	0.4
INDIA (0.0)	0.0% 0.0	0.0% 0.0	0.0% 0.0	0.0% 0.0	0.0% 0.0	0.0% 0.0		0.0% 0.0	0.0% 0.0		0.0% 0.0	0.0% 0.0	0.0% 0.0	0.0% 0.0	0.0% 0.0	0.0% 0.0	0.0% 0.0	0.0% 0.0	0.0% 0.0	0% 0.0	1.6	1.6
MALAYSIA (7.7)	0.0% 0.0	0.0% 0.0	0.0% 0.0	0.0% 0.0	0.0% 0.0	0.0% 0.0		0.0% 0.0	0.0% 0.0	0.0% 0.0		0.0% 0.0	0.0% 0.0	0.0% 0.0	0.0% 0.0	0.0% 0.0	0.0% 0.0	0.0% 0.0	0.0% 0.0	0% 0.0	3.0	10.6
SYRIA (4.8)	0.0% 0.0	0.0% 0.0	0.0% 0.0	0.0% 0.0	0.0% 0.0	0.0% 0.0		0.0% 0.0	0.0% 0.0	0.0% 0.0	0.0% 0.0		0.0% 0.0	0.0% 0.0	0.0% 0.0	0.0% 0.0	0.0% 0.0	0.0% 0.0	0.0% 0.0	0% 0.0	1.3	6.1
TURKEY (4.3)	0.0% 0.0	0.0% 0.0	0.0% 0.0	0.0% 0.0	0.0% 0.0	0.0% 0.0	0.0% 0.0	0.0% 0.0	0.0% 0.0	0.0% 0.0	0.0% 0.0	0.0% 0.0		0.0% 0.0	0.0% 0.0	0.0% 0.0	0.0% 0.0	0.0% 0.0	0.0% 0.0	0% 0.0	0.8	5.0
AMOUNT IMPORTED	0.0	10.5	1.1	0.0	1.7	0.0	0.2	0.0	0.0	1.6	3.0	1.3	0.8	1.1	0.0	0.0	0.0	1.1	0.0	22.1	20.02	47.5

SUM CHECKS

Figure C.9—The First International Transportation Matrix (Cells A25 to AS74)

Figure C.9 shows the next section of the heroin transportation spreadsheet, HEROTRAN.XLS. The user may decide whether to ship heroin from one country to another. Burma's estimated heroin production ready for export (10.5) is presented in cell C9. This value is then carried down to cell A32. Burma is shipping 45 percent of its heroin to Thailand, as indicated in cell E31. Burma is also shipping 10 percent to Laos (cell G31), 15 percent to India (U31), 10 percent to Malaysia (W31), 10 percent to Hong Kong (AC31), and 10 percent to Singapore (AK31). After the user inputs the relevant percentages, formulas will automatically calculate the appropriate amount of heroin that is shipped to each country. (Note: The Source Distribution Table for this matrix is in the range AV52 to BF71.)

TABLE 18. TRANSPORTATION OF HEROIN AMONG "PLAYERS"
(INPUT IN PERCENTS, CONVERTED TO METRIC TONS)

TRANSPORT TO

FROM	BURMA	THAILAND	LAOS	AFGHANISTAN	PAKISTAN	IRAN	MEXICO	GUATEMALA	LEBANON	INDIA	MALAYSIA	SYRIA	TURKEY	HONG KONG	NEPAL	NIGERIA	PHILIPPINES	SINGAPORE	NETHERLANDS	AMOUNT EXPORTED	AMOUNT IMPORTED	AMOUNT REMAINING
BURMA																				0%	0.0	0.0
THAILAND																				100%	0.0	0.0
LAOS																				100%	1.1	0.0
AFGHANISTAN																				0%	0.0	0.0
PAKISTAN																				79%	0.0	0.4
IRAN																				0%	0.0	0.0
MEXICO																				0%	0.0	8.7
GUATEMALA																				0%	0.0	0.0
LEBANON																				0%	0.0	0.4
INDIA																				100%	1.8	1.2
MALAYSIA																				38%	8.2	16.1
SYRIA																				50%	0.0	3.1
TURKEY																				50%	2.3	2.5
HONG KONG																				0%	3.2	4.2
NEPAL																				0%	0.0	0.0
NIGERIA																				0%	8.2	8.2
PHILIPPINES																				0%	0.0	1.1
SINGAPORE																				0%	1.1	1.1
NETHERLANDS																				0%	0.0	8.8
AMOUNT IMPORTED																				29.5	29.5	48.6
																						SUM CHECKS

Figure C.10—The Second International Transportation Matrix (Cells A75 to AS142)

Figure C.10 shows the next section of the heroin transportation spreadsheet, HEROTRAN.XLS. The user may decide whether to ship heroin from one country to another. This matrix functions exactly like the matrix in Figure C.9. (Note: The Source Distribution Table for this matrix is in the range AV119 to BF138.)

	A	B	C	D	E	F	G	H	I	J	K	L	M	N	O	P	Q	R	S	T	U	V	W	X	Y	Z	AA	AC	AE	AG	AI	AK	AM	AO	AQ	AS
143	TABLE 1C. TRANSPORTATION OF HEROIN AMONG "PLAYERS"																																			
144		(INPUT IN PERCENTS, CONVERTED TO METRIC TONS)																																		
145		TRANSPORT TO:																															AMOUNT	AMOUNT	AMOUNT	
146	FROM:	BURMA		THAILAND	LAOS	AFGHANISTAN	PAKISTAN	IRAN	MEXICO	GUATEMALA	LEBANON	INDIA	MALAYSIA	SYRIA	TURKEY	HONG KONG	NEPAL	NIGERIA	PHILIPPINES	SINGAPORE	NETHERLANDS												EXPORTED	IMPORTED	REMAINING

Figure C.11—The Third International Transportation Matrix (Cells A143 to AS209)

Figure C.11 shows the next section of the heroin transportation spreadsheet, HEROTRAN.XLS. The user may decide whether to ship heroin from one country to another. This matrix functions exactly like the matrix in Figure C.9. (Note: The Source Distribution Table for this matrix is in the range AV187 to BF206.)

	A	C	E	G	I	K	M	O	Q	S	U	W	Y	AA	AC	AE	AG	AI	AK	AM	AO	AQ	AS
210	TABLE 1D. TRANSPORTATION OF HEROIN AMONG "PLAYERS"																						
211		(INPUT IN PERCENTS, CONVERTED TO METRIC TONS)																					
212		TRANSPORT TO:																					
213	FROM:	BURMA	THAILAND	LAOS	AFGHANISTAN	PAKISTAN	IRAN	MEXICO	GUATEMALA	LEBANON	INDIA	MALAYSIA	SYRIA	TURKEY	HONG KONG	NEPAL	NIGERIA	PHILIPPINES	SINGAPORE	NETHERLANDS	AMOUNT EXPORTED	AMOUNT IMPORTED	AMOUNT REMAINING
214																							
215	BURMA		0.0%	0.0%	0.0%	0.0%	0.0%	0.0%	0.0%	0.0%	0.0%	0.0%	0.0%	0.0%	0.0%	0.0%	0.0%	0.0%	0.0%	0.0%	0%		
216	0.0		0.0	0.0	0.0	0.0	0.0	0.0	0.0	0.0	0.0	0.0	0.0	0.0	0.0	0.0	0.0	0.0	0.0	0.0	0.0	0.0	0.0
217																							
218	THAILAND	0.0%		0.0%	0.0%	0.0%	0.0%	0.0%	0.0%	0.0%	0.0%	0.0%	0.0%	0.0%	0.0%	0.0%	0.0%	0.0%	0.0%	0.0%	0%		
219	0.0	0.0		0.0	0.0	0.0	0.0	0.0	0.0	0.0	0.0	0.0	0.0	0.0	0.0	0.0	0.0	0.0	0.0	0.0	0.0	0.0	0.0
220																							
221	LAOS	0.0%	0.0%		0.0%	0.0%	0.0%	0.0%	0.0%	0.0%	0.0%	0.0%	0.0%	0.0%	0.0%	0.0%	0.0%	0.0%	0.0%	0.0%	0%		
222	0.0	0.0	0.0		0.0	0.0	0.0	0.0	0.0	0.0	0.0	0.0	0.0	0.0	0.0	0.0	0.0	0.0	0.0	0.0	0.0	0.0	0.0
223																							
224	AFGHANISTAN	0.0%	0.0%	0.0%		0.0%	0.0%	0.0%	0.0%	0.0%	0.0%	0.0%	0.0%	0.0%	0.0%	0.0%	0.0%	0.0%	0.0%	0.0%	0%		
225	0.0	0.0	0.0	0.0		0.0	0.0	0.0	0.0	0.0	0.0	0.0	0.0	0.0	0.0	0.0	0.0	0.0	0.0	0.0	0.0	0.0	0.0
226																							
227	PAKISTAN	0.0%	0.0%	0.0%	0.0%		0.0%	0.0%	0.0%	0.0%	0.0%	0.0%	0.0%	0.0%	0.0%	0.0%	0.0%	0.0%	0.0%	0.0%	0%		
228	0.4	0.0	0.0	0.0	0.0		0.0	0.0	0.0	0.0	0.0	0.0	0.0	0.0	0.0	0.0	0.0	0.0	0.0	0.0	0.0	0.0	0.4
229																							
230	IRAN	0.0%	0.0%	0.0%	0.0%	0.0%		0.0%	0.0%	0.0%	0.0%	0.0%	0.0%	0.0%	0.0%	0.0%	0.0%	0.0%	0.0%	0.0%	0%		
231	0.0	0.0	0.0	0.0	0.0	0.0		0.0	0.0	0.0	0.0	0.0	0.0	0.0	0.0	0.0	0.0	0.0	0.0	0.0	0.0	0.0	0.0
232																							
233	MEXICO	0.0%	0.0%	0.0%	0.0%	0.0%	0.0%		0.0%	0.0%	0.0%	0.0%	0.0%	0.0%	0.0%	0.0%	0.0%	0.0%	0.0%	0.0%	0%		
234	5.7	0.0	0.0	0.0	0.0	0.0	0.0		0.0	0.0	0.0	0.0	0.0	0.0	0.0	0.0	0.0	0.0	0.0	0.0	0.0	0.0	5.7
235																							
236	GUATEMALA	0.0%	0.0%	0.0%	0.0%	0.0%	0.0%	0.0%		0.0%	0.0%	0.0%	0.0%	0.0%	0.0%	0.0%	0.0%	0.0%	0.0%	0.0%	0%		
237	0.0	0.0	0.0	0.0	0.0	0.0	0.0	0.0		0.0	0.0	0.0	0.0	0.0	0.0	0.0	0.0	0.0	0.0	0.0	0.0	0.0	0.0
238																							
239	LEBANON	0.0%	0.0%	0.0%	0.0%	0.0%	0.0%	0.0%	0.0%		0.0%	0.0%	0.0%	0.0%	0.0%	0.0%	0.0%	0.0%	0.0%	0.0%	0%		
240	0.4	0.0	0.0	0.0	0.0	0.0	0.0	0.0	0.0		0.0	0.0	0.0	0.0	0.0	0.0	0.0	0.0	0.0	0.0	0.0	0.0	0.4
241																							
242	INDIA	0.0%	0.0%	0.0%	0.0%	0.0%	0.0%	0.0%	0.0%	0.0%		0.0%	0.0%	0.0%	0.0%	0.0%	0.0%	0.0%	0.0%	0.0%	0%		
243	0.0	0.0	0.0	0.0	0.0	0.0	0.0	0.0	0.0	0.0		0.0	0.0	0.0	0.0	0.0	0.0	0.0	0.0	0.0	0.0	0.0	0.0
244																							
245	MALAYSIA	0.0%	0.0%	0.0%	0.0%	0.0%	0.0%	0.0%	0.0%	0.0%	0.0%		0.0%	0.0%	0.0%	0.0%	0.0%	0.0%	0.0%	0.0%	0%		
246	0.8	0.0	0.0	0.0	0.0	0.0	0.0	0.0	0.0	0.0	0.0		0.0	0.0	0.0	0.0	0.0	0.0	0.0	0.0	0.0	0.0	0.8
247																							
248	SYRIA	0.0%	0.0%	0.0%	0.0%	0.0%	0.0%	0.0%	0.0%	0.0%	0.0%	0.0%		0.0%	0.0%	0.0%	0.0%	0.0%	0.0%	0.0%	0%		
249	3.1	0.0	0.0	0.0	0.0	0.0	0.0	0.0	0.0	0.0	0.0	0.0		0.0	0.0	0.0	0.0	0.0	0.0	0.0	0.0	0.0	3.1
250																							
251	TURKEY	0.0%	0.0%	0.0%	0.0%	0.0%	0.0%	0.0%	0.0%	0.0%	0.0%	0.0%	0.0%		0.0%	0.0%	0.0%	0.0%	0.0%	0.0%	0%		
252	2.5	0.0	0.0	0.0	0.0	0.0	0.0	0.0	0.0	0.0	0.0	0.0	0.0		0.0	0.0	0.0	0.0	0.0	0.0	0.0	0.0	2.5
253																							
254	HONG KONG	0.0%	0.0%	0.0%	0.0%	0.0%	0.0%	0.0%	0.0%	0.0%	0.0%	0.0%	0.0%	0.0%		0.0%	0.0%	0.0%	0.0%	0.0%	0%		
255	18.8	0.0	0.0	0.0	0.0	0.0	0.0	0.0	0.0	0.0	0.0	0.0	0.0	0.0		0.0	0.0	0.0	0.0	0.0	0.0	0.0	18.8
256																							
257	NEPAL	0.0%	0.0%	0.0%	0.0%	0.0%	0.0%	0.0%	0.0%	0.0%	0.0%	0.0%	0.0%	0.0%	0.0%		0.0%	0.0%	0.0%	0.0%	0%		
258	0.0	0.0	0.0	0.0	0.0	0.0	0.0	0.0	0.0	0.0	0.0	0.0	0.0	0.0	0.0		0.0	0.0	0.0	0.0	0.0	0.0	0.0
259																							
260	NIGERIA	0.0%	0.0%	0.0%	0.0%	0.0%	0.0%	0.0%	0.0%	0.0%	0.0%	0.0%	0.0%	0.0%	0.0%	0.0%		0.0%	0.0%	50.0%	50%		
261	10.5	0.0	0.0	0.0	0.0	0.0	0.0	0.0	0.0	0.0	0.0	0.0	0.0	0.0	0.0	0.0		0.0	0.0	5.2	5.2	0.0	5.2
262																							
263	PHILIPPINES	0.0%	0.0%	0.0%	0.0%	0.0%	0.0%	0.0%	0.0%	0.0%	0.0%	0.0%	0.0%	0.0%	0.0%	0.0%	0.0%		0.0%	0.0%	0%		
264	1.1	0.0	0.0	0.0	0.0	0.0	0.0	0.0	0.0	0.0	0.0	0.0	0.0	0.0	0.0	0.0	0.0		0.0	0.0	0.0	0.0	1.1
265																							
266	SINGAPORE	0.0%	0.0%	0.0%	0.0%	0.0%	0.0%	0.0%	0.0%	0.0%	0.0%	0.0%	0.0%	0.0%	0.0%	0.0%	0.0%	0.0%		0.0%	0%		
267	1.1	0.0	0.0	0.0	0.0	0.0	0.0	0.0	0.0	0.0	0.0	0.0	0.0	0.0	0.0	0.0	0.0	0.0		0.0	0.0	0.0	1.1
268																							
269	NETHERLANDS	0.0%	0.0%	0.0%	0.0%	0.0%	0.0%	0.0%	0.0%	0.0%	0.0%	0.0%	0.0%	0.0%	0.0%	0.0%	0.0%	0.0%	0.0%		0%		
270	5.8	0.0	0.0	0.0	0.0	0.0	0.0	0.0	0.0	0.0	0.0	0.0	0.0	0.0	0.0	0.0	0.0	0.0	0.0		0.0	5.2	10.8
271																							
272	AMOUNT																						
273	IMPORTED	0.0	0.0	0.0	0.0	0.0	0.0	0.0	0.0	0.0	0.0	0.0	0.0	0.0	0.0	0.0	0.0	0.0	0.0	5.2	5.2	5.2	49.6
274																							
275																							SUM CHECKS

Figure C.12—The Fourth International Transportation Matrix (Cells A210 to AS275)

Figure C.12 shows the next section of the heroin transportation spreadsheet, HEROTRAN.XLS. The user may decide whether to ship heroin from one country to another. This matrix functions exactly like the matrix in Figure C.9. (Note: The Source Distribution Table for this matrix is in the range AV254 to BF273.)

	A	B	C	D	E	F	G	H	I	J	K	L	M	N	O	P	Q	R
276	TABLE 2: TRANSPORTATION OF HEROIN TO "MARKETS" (COUNTRIES/CONTINENTS)																	
277					(INPUT IN PERCENTS, CONVERTED TO METRIC TONS)													
278							TRANSPORT TO:						SUBTOTAL				ALTERNATIVE	
279					S.E.ASIA/		EUROPE/		TO		UNKNOWN		TO OTHER		AMOUNT		ÁMOUNT	
280	FROM:		CANADA		PACIFIC		MID.EAST		STORAGE		DEST.		MARKETS		TO U.S.		TO U.S.	
281																		
282	BURMA		0.0%		0.0%		0.0%		0.0%		0.0%		0%		100%		#N/A	
283	0.0		0.0		0.0		0.0		0.0		0.0		0.0		0.0			
284																		
285	THAILAND		0.0%		0.0%		0.0%		0.0%		0.0%		0%		100%		#N/A	
286	0.0		0.0		0.0		0.0		0.0		0.0		0.0		0.0			
287																		
288	LAOS		0.0%		0.0%		0.0%		0.0%		0.0%		0%		100%		#N/A	
289	0.0		0.0		0.0		0.0		0.0		0.0		0.0		0.0			
290																		
291	AFGHANISTAN		0.0%		0.0%		0.0%		0.0%		0.0%		0%		100%		#N/A	
292	0.0		0.0		0.0		0.0		0.0		0.0		0.0		0.0			
293																		
294	PAKISTAN		0.0%		0.0%		75.0%		0.0%		0.0%		75%		25%		#N/A	
295	0.4		0.0		0.0		0.3		0.0		0.0		0.3		0.1		#N/A	
296																		
297	IRAN		0.0%		0.0%		0.0%		0.0%		0.0%		0%		100%		#N/A	
298	0.0		0.0		0.0		0.0		0.0		0.0		0.0		0.0			
299																		
300	MEXICO		0.0%		0.0%		0.0%		0.0%		0.0%		0%		100%		#N/A	
301	5.7		0.0		0.0		0.0		0.0		0.0		0.0		5.7		#N/A	
302																		
303	GUATEMALA		0.0%		0.0%		0.0%		0.0%		0.0%		0%		100%		#N/A	
304	0.0		0.0		0.0		0.0		0.0		0.0		0.0		0.0			
305																		
306	LEBANON		0.0%		0.0%		100.0%		0.0%		0.0%		100%		0%		#N/A	
307	0.4		0.0		0.0		0.4		0.0		0.0		0.4		0.0			
308																		
309	INDIA		0.0%		0.0%		0.0%		0.0%		0.0%		0%		100%		#N/A	
310	0.0		0.0		0.0		0.0		0.0		0.0		0.0		0.0		#N/A	
311																		
312	MALAYSIA		0.0%		100.0%		0.0%		0.0%		0.0%		100%		0%		#N/A	
313	0.8		0.0		0.8		0.0		0.0		0.0		0.8		0.0		#N/A	
314																		
315	SYRIA		0.0%		0.0%		100.0%		0.0%		0.0%		100%		0%		#N/A	
316	3.1		0.0		0.0		3.1		0.0		0.0		3.1		0.0			
317																		
318	TURKEY		0.0%		0.0%		100.0%		0.0%		0.0%		100%		0%		#N/A	
319	2.5		0.0		0.0		2.5		0.0		0.0		2.5		0.0		#N/A	
320																		
321	HONG KONG		5.0%		90.0%		0.0%		0.0%		0.0%		95%		5%		#N/A	
322	18.6		0.9		16.7		0.0		0.0		0.0		17.6		0.9		#N/A	
323																		
324	NEPAL		0.0%		0.0%		0.0%		0.0%		0.0%		0%		100%		#N/A	
325	0.0		0.0		0.0		0.0		0.0		0.0		0.0		0.0			
326																		
327	NIGERIA		0.0%		0.0%		50.0%		0.0%		0.0%		50%		50%		#N/A	
328	5.2		0.0		0.0		2.6		0.0		0.0		2.6		2.6		#N/A	
329																		
330	PHILIPPINES		0.0%		90.0%		0.0%		0.0%		0.0%		90%		10%		#N/A	
331	1.1		0.0		1.0		0.0		0.0		0.0		1.0		0.1		#N/A	
332																		
333	SINGAPORE		0.0%		100.0%		0.0%		0.0%		0.0%		100%		0%		#N/A	
334	1.1		0.0		1.1		0.0		0.0		0.0		1.1		0.0		#N/A	
335																		
336	NETHERLANDS		5.0%		0.0%		85.0%		0.0%		0.0%		90%		10%		#N/A	
337	10.8		0.5		0.0		9.2		0.0		0.0		9.7		1.1		#N/A	
338																		
339	TOTALS		1.5		19.5		18.1		0.0		0.0		39.1		10.5		#N/A	
340			Canada		SEA/Pacific		EUR/ME		Storage		Unknown		Subtotal		U.S.		Alternate to U.S.	
341			3.0%		39.3%		36.6%		0.0%		0.0%				21.2%			
342																		
343																		
344																		
345	TABLE 3: FOREIGN SEIZURES																	
346		10.51	estimated Metric Tons headed for the U.S. market BEFORE foreign seizures.															
347		0.845	estimated Metric Tons destined for the U.S. but seized in foreign locations.															
348		8.04%	of the total that is destined for U.S. but is seized in foreign locations.															
349		9.66	estimated Metric Tons headed for the U.S. market AFTER foreign seizures.															
350																		

Figure C.13—Transportation of Heroin to "Markets" and Foreign Seizures
(Cells A276 to R350)

Figure C.13 shows the next section of the heroin transportation spreadsheet, HEROTRAN.XLS. The user may decide to which markets to send a country's heroin. Alternately, the user may ignore the other markets and input only the amount destined for the United States in column Q. Mexico's estimated heroin production ready for shipment to the world's markets (5.7) is presented in cell A301. In the first method, this heroin can be allocated to the world's markets by placing a percentage in cells C300 for Canada, E300 for Southeast Asia and the Pacific, G300 for Europe and the Middle East, I300 for storage, K300 for an unknown destination, and O300 for the United States. One can see, for example, the current estimate that 100 percent of Mexico's heroin is shipped to the United States, as indicated in cell O300. The total amount of heroin shipped to the United States (10.5) by all countries is presented in cell O339, which represents 21.2 percent of all heroin shipped to market (cell O341). The estimate of 10.5 metric tons is carried down to cell A346. The user may then provide an estimate of how much heroin destined for the United States is seized in *foreign locations* (0.845), as shown in cell A347. This amount is subtracted from the system and the resulting net amount remaining (9.66) is provided in cell A349.

84

	A	B	C	D	E	F	G	H	I	J	K	L	M	N	O	P	Q	R
351																		
352																		
353	TABLE 4: DISTRIBUTION OF INCOMING HEROIN AMONG U.S. ENTRY REGIONS																	
354					(INPUT IN PERCENTS, CONVERTED TO METRIC TONS)													
355							TRANSPORT TO:											
356			NORTH-		NORTH-		SOUTH-		SOUTH-		SOUTH-				AMOUNT			
357	FROM:		CENTRAL		EAST		EAST		CENTRAL		WEST		WEST		REMAINING		CHECKSUM	
358																		
359	BURMA		25.0%		50.0%		0.0%		0.0%		0.0%		25.0%		0%		100.0%	
360	0.0		0.0		0.0		0.0		0.0		0.0		0.0		0.0			
361																		
362	THAILAND		0.0%		50.0%		0.0%		0.0%		0.0%		50.0%		0%		100.0%	
363	0.0		0.0		0.0		0.0		0.0		0.0		0.0		0.0			
364																		
365	LAOS		0.0%		50.0%		0.0%		0.0%		0.0%		50.0%		0%		100.0%	
366	0.0		0.0		0.0		0.0		0.0		0.0		0.0		0.0			
367																		
368	AFGHANISTAN		0.0%		50.0%		25.0%		15.0%		0.0%		10.0%		0%		100.0%	
369	0.0		0.0		0.0		0.0		0.0		0.0		0.0		0.0			
370																		
371	PAKISTAN		20.0%		50.0%		20.0%		10.0%		0.0%		0.0%		0%		100.0%	
372	0.1		0.0		0.0		0.0		0.0		0.0		0.0		0.0			
373																		
374	IRAN		0.0%		50.0%		25.0%		15.0%		0.0%		10.0%		0%		100.0%	
375	0.0		0.0		0.0		0.0		0.0		0.0		0.0		0.0			
376																		
377	MEXICO		0.0%		0.0%		0.0%		0.0%		25.0%		75.0%		0%		100.0%	
378	5.2		0.0		0.0		0.0		0.0		1.3		3.9		0.0			
379																		
380	GUATEMALA		0.0%		0.0%		0.0%		0.0%		50.0%		50.0%		0%		100.0%	
381	0.0		0.0		0.0		0.0		0.0		0.0		0.0		0.0			
382																		
383	LEBANON		100.0%		0.0%		0.0%		0.0%		0.0%		0.0%		0%		100.0%	
384	0.0		0.0		0.0		0.0		0.0		0.0		0.0		0.0			
385																		
386	INDIA		10.0%		50.0%		10.0%		10.0%		10.0%		10.0%		0%		100.0%	
387	0.0		0.0		0.0		0.0		0.0		0.0		0.0		0.0			
388																		
389	MALAYSIA		16.7%		16.7%		16.7%		16.7%		16.7%		16.7%		0%		100.0%	
390	0.0		0.0		0.0		0.0		0.0		0.0		0.0		0.0			
391																		
392	SYRIA		100.0%		0.0%		0.0%		0.0%		0.0%		0.0%		0%		100.0%	
393	0.0		0.0		0.0		0.0		0.0		0.0		0.0		0.0			
394																		
395	TURKEY		16.7%		16.7%		16.7%		16.7%		16.7%		16.7%		0%		100.0%	
396	0.0		0.0		0.0		0.0		0.0		0.0		0.0		0.0			
397																		
398	HONG KONG		25.0%		25.0%		0.0%		0.0%		0.0%		50.0%		0%		100.0%	
399	0.9		0.2		0.2		0.0		0.0		0.0		0.4		0.0			
400																		
401	NEPAL		0.0%		100.0%		0.0%		0.0%		0.0%		0.0%		0%		100.0%	
402	0.0		0.0		0.0		0.0		0.0		0.0		0.0		0.0			
403																		
404	NIGERIA		30.0%		50.0%		10.0%		10.0%		0.0%		0.0%		0%		100.0%	
405	2.4		0.7		1.2		0.2		0.2		0.0		0.0		0.0			
406																		
407	PHILIPPINES		0.0%		0.0%		0.0%		0.0%		0.0%		100.0%		0%		100.0%	
408	0.1		0.0		0.0		0.0		0.0		0.0		0.1		0.0			
409																		
410	SINGAPORE		16.7%		16.7%		16.7%		16.7%		16.7%		16.7%		0%		100.0%	
411	0.0		0.0		0.0		0.0		0.0		0.0		0.0		0.0			
412																		
413	NETHERLANDS		20.0%		50.0%		20.0%		10.0%		0.0%		0.0%		0%		100.0%	
414	1.0		0.2		0.5		0.2		0.1		0.0		0.0		0.0			
415																		
416																		
417	9.66 (mt) into the U.S. before DOMESTIC seizures and after FOREIGN seizures.																	
418																		

Figure C.14—Distribution of Incoming Heroin Among U.S. Entry Regions
(Cells A351 to R418)

Figure C.14 shows the next section of the heroin transportation spreadsheet, HEROTRAN.XLS. The user may decide to which of the six U.S. entry regions to send a country's heroin. In the example shown, Mexico has 5.2 metric tons in cell A378 carried down from the previous table. In this example, we have specified that 25 percent is shipped to the Southwest region (cell K377) and 75 percent is shipped the West region (cell M377).

	A	B	C	D	E	F	G	H	I	J	K	L	M	N	O	P
419	**TABLE 5A. DISTRIBUTION OF TRANSPORTATION MODES INTO U.S. ENTRY REGIONS**															
420					*IN PERCENTS--DEFAULT TABLE*											
421			NORTH-		NORTH-		SOUTH-		SOUTH-		SOUTH-					
422			CENTRAL		EAST		EAST		CENTRAL		WEST		WEST			
423																
424	COMMERCIAL		100%		100%		100%		50%		39%		27%			
425	AIR															
426																
427	PRIVATE		0%		0%		0%		0%		0%		0%			
428	AIR															
429																
430	COMMERCIAL		0%		0%						0%		0%			
431	LAND						XXX		XXX							
432																
433	PRIVATE		0%		0%						61%		1%			
434	LAND						XXX		XXX							
435																
436	COMMERCIAL		0%		0%		0%		50%		0%		72%			
437	SEA															
438																
439	PRIVATE		0%		0%		0%		0%		0%		0%			
440	SEA															
441																
442	CHECKSUM		100.0%		100.0%		100.0%		100.0%		100.0%		100.0%			
443																
444																
445	**TABLE 5B. DISTRIBUTION OF TRANSPORTATION MODES INTO U.S. ENTRY REGIONS**															
446					*IN PERCENTS--ALTERNATIVE TABLE*											
447	NOTE: The column percentage must equal 100%. Otherwise, none of the cell percentages in that column will be used.															
448			NORTH-		NORTH-		SOUTH-		SOUTH-		SOUTH-					
449			CENTRAL		EAST		EAST		CENTRAL		WEST		WEST			
450																
451	COMMERCIAL		0%		0%		0%		0%		0%		0%			
452	AIR															
453																
454	PRIVATE		0%		0%		0%		0%		0%		0%			
455	AIR															
456																
457	COMMERCIAL		0%		0%						0%		0%			
458	LAND						XXX		XXX							
459																
460	PRIVATE		0%		0%						0%		0%			
461	LAND						XXX		XXX							
462																
463	COMMERCIAL		0%		0%		0%		0%		0%		0%			
464	SEA															
465																
466	PRIVATE		0%		0%		0%		0%		0%		0%			
467	SEA															
468																
469	TOTAL		NOT 100%		NOT 100%		NOT 100%		NOT 100%		NOT 100%		NOT 100%			
470																
471																
472																

Figure C.15—Distribution of Transportation Modes into U.S. Entry Regions
(Cells A419 to P472)

Figure C.15 shows the next section of the heroin transportation spreadsheet, HEROTRAN.XLS. The user may decide on the transportation modes of the heroin into the six U.S. entry regions. In the example shown, 100 percent of the heroin entering the North Central region arrives through commercial air (cell C424). All of the percentages in Table 5A are derived automatically from seizure data in Table 6. Alternatively, the user can input other data in Table 5B. If any data are provided by the user in Table 5B, they will be used instead of the percentages in Table 5A. However, the user must ensure that the column percentages total 100 percent. Otherwise, none of the percentages in that column will be recognized by the model.

	A	B	C	D	E	F	G	H	I	J	K	L	M	N	O	P
473	TABLE 6. SEIZURES OF HEROIN (TRANSPORTATION MODE BY U.S. ENTRY REGION)															
474							*IN METRIC TONS*									
475			NORTH-		NORTH-		SOUTH-		SOUTH-		SOUTH-				TOTAL	
476			CENTRAL		EAST		EAST		CENTRAL		WEST		WEST		BY MODE	
477																
478	COMMERCIAL															
479	AIR		0.201		1.129		0.016		0.000		0.016		0.238		1.5990	
480																
481	PRIVATE															
482	AIR		0.000		0.000		0.000		0.000		0.000		0.000		0.0000	
483																
484	COMMERCIAL						---		---							
485	LAND		0.000		0.000						0.000		0.000		0.0000	
486																
487	PRIVATE						---		---							
488	LAND		0.000		0.000						0.024		0.008		0.0324	
489																
490	COMMERCIAL															
491	SEA		0.000		0.000		0.000		0.000		0.000		0.628		0.6280	
492																
493	PRIVATE															
494	SEA		0.000		0.000		0.000		0.000		0.000		0.000		0.0000	
495																
496	TOTAL														2.259	
497	BY REGION		0.201		1.129		0.016		0.000		0.040		0.874		2.259	
498			8.9%		50.0%		0.7%		0.0%		1.8%		38.7%			
499																

Figure C.16—Seizures of Heroin (Cells A473 to P498)

Figure C.16 shows the next section of the heroin transportation spreadsheet, HEROTRAN.XLS. The user may decide on the amount of heroin that is seized by entry region and transportation mode. In the example shown, a total of 2.259 metric tons are seized (cell O496, O497). In the Northeast, for instance, 1.129 metric tons are seized by commercial air (cell E479).

	A	B	C	D	E	F	G	H	I	J	K	L	M
1													
2					UNITED STATES DISTRIBUTION: HEROIN								
3					YEAR=		1991						
4													
5	TABLE 1.	HEROIN COMING INTO THE UNITED STATES											
6				BY REGION (MTs)									
7													
8													
9			Net of POE		Domestic				Alternate				
10			seizures.		Production		TOTAL		TOTAL				
11	-------------------		---------------		-----------------		---------------		------------------				
12	NORTH-												
13	CENTRAL		0.95		0.00		0.95		#N/A				
14	-------------------		---------------		-----------------		---------------		------------------				
15	NORTH-												
16	EAST		0.83		0.00		0.83		#N/A				
17	-------------------		---------------		-----------------		---------------		------------------				
18	SOUTH-												
19	EAST		0.44		0.00		0.44		#N/A				
20	-------------------		---------------		-----------------		---------------		------------------				
21	SOUTH-												
22	CENTRAL		0.35		0.00		0.35		#N/A				
23	-------------------		---------------		-----------------		---------------		------------------				
24	SOUTH-												
25	WEST		1.26		0.00		1.26		#N/A				
26	-------------------		---------------		-----------------		---------------		------------------				
27													
28	WEST		3.56		0.00		3.56		#N/A				
29	-------------------		---------------		-----------------		---------------		------------------				
30							7.40		#N/A				
31	TOTAL		7.40		0.00		7.40						
32													
33													

Figure C.17—Heroin Coming into the United States (Cells A1 to M33)

Figure C.17 shows the first section of the heroin U.S. distribution spreadsheet, HEROUSA.XLS. The user may decide on the regional domestic production totals. There is also a column for the user to input an alternative total. In the example shown, 0.95 metric ton is coming into the North Central region (after foreign and point of entry into the U.S. seizures), and is reflected in cell C13. The numbers in this column are linked to HEROTRAN.XLS.

	A	E	C	D	E	F	G	H	I	J	K	L	M	N	O		Q		S	T
34	TABLE 2.		INTER-REGIONAL TRANSFERS OF HEROIN																	
35			*(INPUT IN PERCENTS, CONVERTED TO METRIC TONS)*																	
36			*TRANSFER TO:*																	
37	TRANSFER		N. CENT		N. EAST		S. EAST		S. CENT		S. WEST		WEST		Transfers		Transfers		Amount	
38	FROM:		CENTRAL		EAST		EAST		CENTRAL		WEST		WEST		OUT		IN		REMAINING	
39	*FROM*																			
40	N. CENTRAL				0%		0%		0%		0%		10%		10%					
41		1.0			0.0		0.0		0.0		0.0		0.1		0.1		0.9		1.7	
42																				
43	N. EAST		5%				0.0%		5.0%		5.0%		0%		15%					
44		0.8	0.0				0.0		0.0		0.0		0.0		0.1		1.4		2.1	
45																				
46	S. EAST		10%		50%				5%		10%		10%		85%					
47		0.4	0.0		0.2				0.0		0.0		0.0		0.4		0.2		0.2	
48																				
49	S. CENTRAL		0%		0%		10%				25%		50%		85%					
50		0.3	0.0		0.0		0.0				0.1		0.2		0.3		0.5		0.5	
51																				
52	S. WEST		5%		20%		10%		5%				10%		50%					
53		1.3	0.1		0.3		0.1		0.1				0.1		0.6		0.5		1.2	
54																				
55	WEST		20%		25%		0%		10%		10%				65%					
56		3.6	0.7		0.9		0.0		0.4		0.4				2.3		0.4		1.7	
57																				
58																				

Figure C.18—Interregional Transfers of Heroin (Cells A34 to T58)

Figure C.18 shows the next section of the heroin U.S. distribution spreadsheet, HEROUSA.XLS. The user may decide on the interregional domestic transfers of heroin. In this example, 5 percent of the heroin shipped into the Northeast region is shipped again to the North Central region, as shown in cell C43.

	A	B	C	D	E	F	G	H	I	J	K	L
59												
60	TABLE 3.		DOMESTIC SEIZURES OF HEROIN (NON-POE)									
61												
62	Gross Amount in each Region				--Minus--				Net Amount in each Region			
63	Ready for Sales (kgs.)						Other		Ready for Sales (kgs.)			
64					Seizures		Losses					
65	N. CENTRAL		1,716		0.32		0		1,716			
66	N. EAST		2,070		2.56		0		2,067			
67	S. EAST		228		0.32		0		227			
68	S. CENTRAL		535		0.32		0		535			
69	S. WEST		1,162		0.32		0		1,161			
70	WEST		1,687		2.20		0		1,685			
71	TOTAL								TOTAL			
72			7,398		6.06		0		7,392			
73												
74												
75												
76	TABLE 4.		REGIONAL DISTRIBUTION OF NET HEROIN READY FOR SALES									
77			(INPUT IN PERCENTS, CONVERTED TO KILOGRAMS)									
78												
79	NORTH-CENTRAL											
80	CHICAGO (II)		0%		0							
81	DETROIT (II)		0%		0							
82	ALL OTHER		100%		1,716							
83												
84	NORTH-EAST											
85	BOSTON (II)		0%		0							
86	NEWARK (II)		0%		0							
87	NEW YORK (I)		0%		0							
88	ALL OTHER		100%		2,067							
89												
90	SOUTH-EAST											
91	ATLANTA		0%		0							
92	MIAMI (I)		0%		0							
93	ALL OTHER		100%		227							
94												
95	SOUTH-CENTRAL											
96	NEW ORLEANS		0%		0							
97	ALL OTHER		100%		535							
98												
99	SOUTH-WEST											
100	EL PASO (~I)		0%		0							
101	HOUSTON (I)		0%		0							
102	ALL OTHER		100%		1,161							
103												
104	WEST											
105	LOS ANGELES (I)		0%		0							
106	SAN DIEGO (II)		0%		0							
107	SAN FRANCISCO (II)		0%		0							
108	SEATTLE		0%		0							
109	ALL OTHER		100%		1,685							
110												
111	TOTAL				7,392							

Figure C.19—State and Local Seizures and the Regional Distribution of Net Heroin Ready for Sale (Cells A59 to L111)

Figure C.19 shows the next section of the heroin U.S. distribution spreadsheet, HEROUSA.XLS. The user may decide on the amount of heroin to be withdrawn from the system by state and local seizures, and if desired, the amount of heroin to ship to some major cities. Domestic seizures are withdrawn from the system by inputting values in cells E65 to E70. Also, other losses can be taken from the system in cells G65 to G70. If the user desires to allocate the heroin to some major cities, this is accomplished by placing the percentage value in cells C80–81, C85–87, C91–92, C96, C100–101, and/or C105–108.

	A	B	C	D	E	F	G	H	I	J	K	L	M	N
112														
113	TABLE 5A. DRUG MARKET HIERARCHY--DEFAULT TABLE													
114					*IN KILOGRAMS PER ANNUM*									
115			NORTH-		NORTH-		SOUTH-		SOUTH-		SOUTH-			
116			CENTRAL		EAST		EAST		CENTRAL		WEST		WEST	
117	----------------		----------------		----------------		----------------		----------------		----------------		----------------	
118	Distributors		0.0		0.0		0.0		0.0		0.0		0.0	
119														
120	----------------		----------------		----------------		----------------		----------------		----------------		----------------	
121	Wholesalers		0.0		0.0		0.0		0.0		0.0		0.0	
122														
123	----------------		----------------		----------------		----------------		----------------		----------------		----------------	
124	Street Dealer		0.0		0.0		0.0		0.0		0.0		0.0	
125														
126	----------------		----------------		----------------		----------------		----------------		----------------		----------------	
127	USERS		0.039		0.039		0.039		0.039		0.039		0.039	
128														
129	----------------		----------------		----------------		----------------		----------------		----------------		----------------	
130														
131														
132	----------------		----------------		----------------		----------------		----------------		----------------		----------------	
133														
134														
135	TABLE 5B. DRUG MARKET HIERARCHY--ALTERNATIVE TABLE													
136					*IN KILOGRAMS PER ANNUM*									
137			NORTH-		NORTH-		SOUTH-		SOUTH-		SOUTH-			
138			CENTRAL		EAST		EAST		CENTRAL		WEST		WEST	
139	----------------		----------------		----------------		----------------		----------------		----------------		----------------	
140	Distributors		#N/A		#N/A		#N/A		#N/A		#N/A		#N/A	
141														
142	----------------		----------------		----------------		----------------		----------------		----------------		----------------	
143	Wholesalers		#N/A		#N/A		#N/A		#N/A		#N/A		#N/A	
144														
145	----------------		----------------		----------------		----------------		----------------		----------------		----------------	
146	Street Dealer		#N/A		#N/A		#N/A		#N/A		#N/A		#N/A	
147														
148	----------------		----------------		----------------		----------------		----------------		----------------		----------------	
149	USERS:		#N/A		#N/A		#N/A		#N/A		#N/A		#N/A	
150														
151	----------------		----------------		----------------		----------------		----------------		----------------		----------------	
152														
153														
154	----------------		----------------		----------------		----------------		----------------		----------------		----------------	
155														

Figure C.20—Drug Market Hierarchy Tables (Cells A112 to N155)

Figure C.20 shows the next section of the heroin U.S. distribution spreadsheet, HEROUSA.XLS. The user may input an estimate of the average amount of heroin consumed. The default table (5A) shows only data for users and indicates that 0.039 kg is the average value. This is presented in cells C127, E127, G127, I127, K127, and M127. The alternative table, Table 5B, allows the user to input his or her own values. Any values placed in this table override the values in Table 5A. If the user desires to input an alternative amount of average use, these values can be input into cells C149, E149, G149, I149, K149, and M149.

	A	B	C	D	E	F	G	H	I	J	K	L	M	N
156	TABLE 6.		PURITY LEVELS		Purity at Purchase									
157														
158			NORTH-		NORTH-		SOUTH-		SOUTH-		SOUTH-			
159			CENTRAL		EAST		EAST		CENTRAL		WEST		WEST	
160	--------		--------		--------		--------		--------		--------		--------	
161	Distributors		100.0%		100.0%		100.0%		100.0%		100.0%		100.0%	
162														
163	--------		--------		--------		--------		--------		--------		--------	
164	Wholesalers		100.0%		100.0%		100.0%		100.0%		70.0%		70.0%	
165														
166	--------		--------		--------		--------		--------		--------		--------	
167	Street Dealer		75.0%		75.0%		75.0%		75.0%		50.0%		50.0%	
168														
169	--------		--------		--------		--------		--------		--------		--------	
170	USERS:		30.0%		30.0%		30.0%		30.0%		30.0%		30.0%	
171														
172	--------		--------		--------		--------		--------		--------		--------	
173														

Figure C.21—Purity Levels (Cells A156 to N173)

Figure C.21 shows the next section of the heroin U.S. distribution spreadsheet, HEROUSA.XLS. The user may input an estimate of the average purity level of the heroin at different levels in the market. In this case, the average purity levels for users (as opposed to distributors, wholesalers, or dealers) is 30 percent (see cells C170, E170, G170, I170, K170, and M170).

TABLE 7. DRUG MARKET POPULATION DATA

	Distributor	Wholesaler	Street Dealers	USERS: (in 000s)	Population (in 000s)	Calculated Prevalence	N.H.S. Prevalence Past Year	95% Confidence Interval Low	High	RATIO
NORTH CENTRAL										
CHICAGO (II)	#DIV/0!	#DIV/0!	#DIV/0!	0	0	NA	0.3%			NA
DETROIT (II)	#DIV/0!	#DIV/0!	#DIV/0!	0	0	NA	0.3%			NA
ALL OTHER	#DIV/0!	#DIV/0!	#DIV/0!	146	58,031	0.3%	0.3%	0.4%	1.3%	0.85
NORTHEAST										
BOSTON (II)	#DIV/0!	#DIV/0!	#DIV/0!	0	0	NA	0.7%			NA
NEWARK (II)	#DIV/0!	#DIV/0!	#DIV/0!	0	0	NA	0.7%			NA
NEW YORK (I)	#DIV/0!	#DIV/0!	#DIV/0!	0	0	NA	0.7%			NA
ALL OTHER	#DIV/0!	#DIV/0!	#DIV/0!	175	47,152	0.4%	0.7%	0.6%	1.8%	0.57
SOUTHEAST										
ATLANTA	#DIV/0!	#DIV/0!	#DIV/0!	0	0	NA	0.2%			NA
MIAMI (I)	#DIV/0!	#DIV/0!	#DIV/0!	0	0	NA	0.2%			NA
ALL OTHER	#DIV/0!	#DIV/0!	#DIV/0!	19	30,996	0.1%	0.2%	0.4%	1.1%	0.31
SOUTH CENTRAL										
NEW ORLEANS	#DIV/0!	#DIV/0!	#DIV/0!	0	0	NA	0.2%			NA
ALL OTHER	#DIV/0!	#DIV/0!	#DIV/0!	45	14,860	0.3%	0.2%	0.4%	1.1%	1.53
SOUTHWEST										
EL PASO (-I)	#DIV/0!	#DIV/0!	#DIV/0!	0	0	NA	0.2%			NA
HOUSTON (I)	#DIV/0!	#DIV/0!	#DIV/0!	0	0	NA	0.2%			NA
ALL OTHER	#DIV/0!	#DIV/0!	#DIV/0!	98	19,900	0.5%	0.2%	0.4%	1.3%	2.25
WEST										
LOS ANGELES (I)	#DIV/0!	#DIV/0!	#DIV/0!	0	0	NA	0.3%			NA
SAN DIEGO (II)	#DIV/0!	#DIV/0!	#DIV/0!	0	0	NA	0.3%			NA
SAN FRANCISCO (III)	#DIV/0!	#DIV/0!	#DIV/0!	0	0	NA	0.3%			NA
SEATTLE	#DIV/0!	#DIV/0!	#DIV/0!	0	0	NA	0.3%			NA
ALL OTHER	#DIV/0!	#DIV/0!	#DIV/0!	143	30,193	0.5%	0.3%	0.5%	2.0%	1.58
US TOTAL	#DIV/0!	#DIV/0!	#DIV/0!	627	201,131	0.3%	0.3%	0.6%	1.1%	1.04

Figure C.22—Drug Market Population Data (Cells A174 to V213)

Figure C.22 shows the last section of the heroin U.S. distribution spreadsheet, HEROUSA.XLS. The user must ensure that the population numbers presented in column M are basically correct. These figures are based on 1990 census data. The estimated number of users is presented in column I. These percentages are compared to the population numbers in column M to obtain the calculated prevalence percentage shown in column O. This percentage can be compared to the National Household Survey percentage presented in column Q. Finally, the ratio in column U is the ratio of the model's calculated prevalence to the Household Survey's estimated prevalence.

D. A Short Primer on the INCSR's Data Collection Methodology

In this appendix, we present a verbatim portion of the 1991 *International Narcotics Control Strategy Report* that discusses the methodology for estimating various factors in illegal drug production. It identifies the estimates in which there is the least (and most) certainty as well as some of the reasons for the differences in certainty.[1] This discussion is applicable to cocaine, heroin, and marijuana.

> **Methodology for Estimating Illegal Drug Production: How much do we know?** This report [1991 INCSR] contains tables showing a variety of illicit narcotics-related data. While these numbers represent the United States Government's (USG) best effort to sketch the dimensions of the inter- national drug problem, the reader should be aware that the picture is not always as precise as we would like it to be. The numbers range from cultivation figures, hard data derived by proven means, to crop production and drug yield estimates, where many more variables come into play. Since much information is lacking where yields are concerned, the numbers are subject to revision as more data becomes known.

> **What we know with reasonable certainty:** The most reliable information we have on illicit drugs is how many hectares are under cultivation. For more than a decade, the USG has estimated the extent of illicit cultivation in a dozen nations using proven methods similar to those used to estimate the size of licit crops at home and abroad. We can thus estimate the size of crops with reasonable accuracy.

> **What we know with less certainty:** Where crop yields are concerned, the picture is less clear. How much of a finished product a given area will pro- duce is difficult to estimate, since small changes in such factors as soil fertility, weather, farming techniques, and disease can produce widely varying results from year to year and place to place. In addition, most illicit drug crop areas are inaccessible to the USG, making scientific information difficult to obtain. Moreover, we must stress that even as we refine our methods of analysis, we are estimating *potential* crop available for harvest. These estimates do not allow for losses, which could represent anything from a tenth to a third (or more) of a crop in some areas for some harvests. Thus, the estimate of the potential crop is useful in providing comparative analysis from year to year, but the actual quantity of final product remains elusive.

> **Harvest Estimates:** Estimating the quantities of coca leaf, opium gum, and marijuana actually harvested and available for processing into finished narcotics remains a major challenge. *We currently cannot accurately estimate this amount for any illicit crop in any nation.* While farmers naturally have strong incentives to maximize their harvests of what is almost always their

---

[1]Refer to the *International Narcotics Control Strategy Report,* United States, Department of State, March 1991, pp. 7–8.

most profitable cash crop, the harvest depends upon the efficiency of farming practices and the wastage caused by poor practices or difficult weather conditions during and after harvest. A tenth to a third (or more) of a crop may be lost in some areas during harvests. Additional information and analysis may enable us to make adjustments for these factors in the future. Similar deductions for local consumption of unprocessed coca leaf and opium may be possible as well through the accumulation of additional information and research.

Processing Estimates. The wide variation in processing efficiencies achieved by traffickers complicates the task of estimating the quantity of cocaine or heroin which could be refined from a crop. These efficiencies vary because of differences in the origin and quality of the raw material used, the technical processing method employed, the size and sophistication of laboratories, and the skill and experience of local workers and chemists. The USG continues to estimate potential cocaine production as a range based on processing efficiencies that appear to be most common.

The actual amount of dry coca leaf or opium converted into a final product during any time period remains unknown, given the possible losses noted earlier. There are indications, however, that cocaine processing efficiencies improved during the 1980s, and that traffickers still have considerable room for improvement.

Figures will change as techniques and data quality improve. The reader may ask: are this year's figures definitive? The reply is, almost certainly, some are not. Additional research may result in future revision to USG estimates of potential drug production. For the present, however, these statistics represent the state of the art. As the art improves, so will the precision of the estimates.

E. A Simulation to Test for the Effect of Propagating Errors in the Model

Because of the high number of parameters in the model and the likelihood that most are estimated with some degree of error, there is the possibility that even slight errors in parameter values can propagate throughout the system and translate into large errors in the later stages of the model. We conducted a simulation to test the model's robustness in the face of these propagating errors. We chose six parameters and randomly changed each by an amount within 20 percent of the initial value.[1] Then, we compared the model's estimated number of users from each of the 50 iterations to the model's beginning value.[2]

The six parameters are taken from each of the model's spreadsheets (i.e., production, transportation, and domestic distribution) and are representative of all of the model's parameters in terms of their impact on the model's output. In other words, some parameters have a large influence on the model's output while others have relatively little impact. The six parameters are:

- Burma Opium Yield Factor (metric tons of opium per hectare)—Burma constitutes about 68 percent of the estimated hectares of opium under cultivation for 1991.[3] The sensitivity analysis presented in Table E.1 reveals that this parameter exercises a significant impact on the model's output. For example, a 50 percent change in this parameter results in an 71 percent change in the estimated number of users.

- Burma Opium Consumption (metric tons)—Approximately 150 metric tons were consumed in Burma during 1991, making it the largest domestic consumer of opium among the nine producing countries included in the model. However, it is likely that this parameter has an insignificant influence on the model's output. For example, as presented in Table 4.1, Laos's opium consumption is about 29 metric tons, and a 50 percent change in this parameter results in a 2.3 percent change in the estimated number of users.

---

[1]We used Excel's random number generator to create a table of random numbers that ranged in value from −20 percent to +20 percent. The 20 percent figure is somewhat arbitrary but we believe an appropriate amount for this illustrative exercise.

[2]Any propagating errors would ostensibly find their greatest impact at the end of the model, so we decided to use the estimated number of users, because it is the final model estimate.

[3]This includes Burma, Thailand, Laos, Afghanistan, Pakistan, Iran, Lebanon, Mexico, and Guatemala.

Table E.1

Output from the Simulation

Iteration	Users (000)	Iter.	Users (000)	Iter.	Users (000)	Iter.	Users (000)	Iter.	Users (000)
1	953	11	677	21	589	31	506	41	838
2	926	12	650	22	617	32	682	42	807
3	769	13	595	23	680	33	522	43	558
4	479	14	725	24	543	34	418	44	660
5	530	15	561	25	632	35	1,132	45	442
6	454	16	632	26	625	36	592	46	649
7	540	17	544	27	841	37	609	47	554
8	1,055	18	402	28	520	38	792	48	547
9	574	19	687	29	706	39	546	49	580
10	842	20	654	30	647	40	944	50	641

- Foreign Seizures (metric tons)—With less than one metric ton of heroin removed from the system, it is likely that this parameter will have a negligible impact on the model's output.

- Average Purity—This parameter can have a major influence over the model's output. Indeed, the sensitivity analysis presented in Table 4.1 reveals that a 50 percent change in this parameter results in a 33 percent change in the estimated number of users.

- Domestic Seizures (metric tons)—Since only about 6 metric tons of heroin are extracted from the system in 1991, it is likely that this parameter will have a minor effect on the model's output.

- Annual Consumption (kilograms)—This parameter can potentially have a major effect on the model's output. The sensitivity analysis in Table 4.1 shows that a 50 percent change in its value results in a 34 percent change in the estimated number of users.

The output from the simulation is presented in Table E.1. The beginning value in the model for the estimated number of users is 627,000.[4] The minimum value obtained is 402 thousand (or 64 percent of the beginning value), the maximum is 1.1 million (181 percent of the beginning value); the median is 628 thousand (100 percent of the beginning value); and the mean is 653 thousand (104 percent of the beginning value).

---

[4]One should not interpret this as our definitive estimate of the number of heroin users in the United States. Rather, it should be interpreted as the number of users there must be *if one accepts all previous parameter estimates in the model.*

106

These data are largely clustered around the beginning value. This is evidenced by the fact that 72 percent of the simulation output is within 25 percent of the beginning value, as illustrated in Figure E.1.

Moreover, these data are more or less uniformly distributed around the beginning value, but some skewing is evident. This is illustrated in Figure E.2.

We conclude from this simulation that the model is generally robust in the face of propagating errors. The vast majority of the simulation output falls close to the beginning value of 627 thousand. Indeed, 72 percent of the simulation output falls within 25 percent of the beginning value. In a limited number of cases, however, the effect of propagating errors produces values that are significantly different from the beginning value. All of this suggests that in most cases (but not all), the errors will countervail each other.

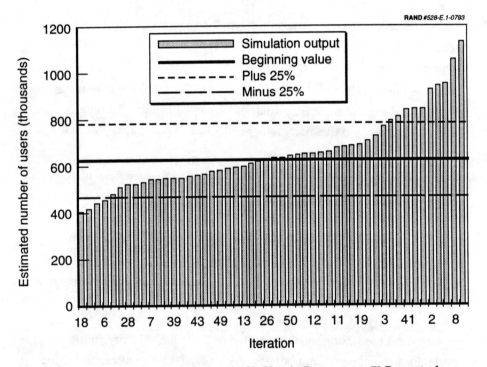

Figure E.1—Fifty Random Changes in Six Heroin Parameters: 72 Percent of Simulation Output Is Within 25 Percent of the Beginning Value

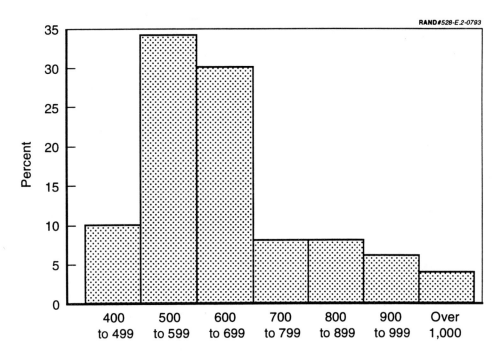

Figure E.2—Histogram of Heroin User Output

Bibliography

Abt Associates, *What America's Users Spend on Illegal Drugs*, technical paper for the ONDCP, June 1991.

BOTEC Analysis Corporation, *Heroin Situation Assessment*, working paper done for the ONDCP, January 10, 1992.

Carpenter, Ted G., and R. Channing Rouse, "Perilous Panacea: The Military in the Drug War," CATO Institute Policy Analysis, No. 128, February 15, 1990.

Cooper, Donald A., "Clandestine Production Processes for Cocaine and Heroin," in *Clandestinely Produced Drugs, Analogues and Precursors*, (proceedings from a conference co-sponsored by the World Health Organization and the Drug Enforcement Administration, September 1987), edited by M. Klein, F. Sapienza, H. McClain, Jr., and I. Khan, 1989.

Dombey-Moore, Bonnie, Susan Resetar, and Michael Childress, *A System Description of the Cocaine Trade*, MR-236-A/AF, RAND, forthcoming.

Hamill and Cooley, "National Estimates of Heroin Prevalence 1980–1987: Results from Analysis of DAWN Emergency Room Data," RTI Technical Report, 1990.

INCSR—See U.S. Department of State.

Krivanek, Jara K., *Heroin: Myths and Reality*, Winchester, Mass.: Allen & Unwin, Inc., 1988.

National Narcotics Consumers Committee, *National Narcotics Intelligence Consumers Committee Report*, various years.

ONDCP—See U.S. Office of National Drug Control Policy.

Reuter, Peter, and David Ronfeldt, *Quest for Integrity: The Mexican-U.S. Drug Issue in the 1980s*, Santa Monica, Calif.: RAND, N-3266-USDP, 1992.

Richburg, Keith B., "Reagan Order Defines Drug Trade as Security Threat," *Washington Post*, June 8, 1986.

Surrett, William Roy, *The International Narcotics Trade: An Overview of Its Dimensions, Production Sources, and Organizations*, Congressional Research Service, October 3, 1988.

Treaster, Joseph B., "Colombia's Drug Lords Sending Heroin to U.S.," *New York Times*, January 14, 1992, p. A10.

Treaster, Joseph B., "Executive's Secret Struggle with Heroin's Powerful Grip," *New York Times*, July 22, 1992.

110

U.S. Congress, House of Representatives, *Asian Heroin Production and Trafficking*, Hearings Before the Select Committee on Narcotics Abuse and Control, August 1, 1989.

U.S. Congress, House of Representatives, *Heroin Trafficking and Abuse: A Growing Crisis*, Hearings Before the Select Committee on Narcotics Abuse and Control, July 19, 1990.

U.S. Congress, House Committee on the Judiciary, *Posse Comitatus Act, Hearing*, 97th Congress, 1st Session, June 3, 1981.

U.S. Department of Health and Human Services, National Institute on Drug Abuse (NIDA), *National Household Survey on Drug Abuse: Population Estimates*, various issues.

U.S. Department of Justice, Drug Enforcement Administration, Office of Intelligence, *Domestic Monitor Program: An Annual Report on the Source Areas, Cost, and Purity of Retail-Level Heroin*, various issues.

U.S. Department of Justice, Drug Enforcement Administration, Office of Intelligence, *From the Source to the Street: Mid-1990 Prices for Cannabis, Cocaine, and Heroin, Intelligence Trends*, various issues.

U.S. Department of Justice, Drug Enforcement Administration, Office of Intelligence, *Worldwide Heroin Situation 1990*, May 1991.

U.S. Department of Justice, Drug Enforcement Administration, Office of Intelligence, *Special Report: Black Tar Heroin in the United States*, March 1986.

U.S. Department of State, *International Narcotics Control Strategy Report*, various issues.

U.S. General Accounting Office, *Drug Law Enforcement: Military Assistance for Anti-Drug Agencies*, GAO/GGD-88-27, December 1987.

U.S. Office of National Drug Control Policy, *National Drug Control Strategy*, various issues.

U.S. Office of National Drug Control Policy, *National Drug Control Strategy: Implementing the President's Plan*, June 1992.

U.S. Office of National Drug Control Policy, *The Heroin Situation: A Status Report*, Bulletin No. 5, April 1992.